NURTURE

How to Make Care
Your Competitive Advantage

Jane Anderson

Copyright © Jane Anderson 2023

All models copyright © Jane Anderson

All rights reserved. No part of this publication may be reproduced by any means without the prior written consent of the publisher.

This book uses stories to enforce the meaning behind its relevant chapter. Permission to use these stories has been provided.

Every effort has been made to trace (and seek permission for use of) the original source of material used within this book. Where the attempt has been unsuccessful, the publisher would be pleased to hear from the author / publisher to rectify any omission.

Cover design: Yna

Editing: Kristen Lowrey

ISBN: 978-0-6485022-2-7 (pbk) eISBN: 978-0-6485022-3-4 (ebook)

 A catalogue record for this book is available from the National Library of Australia

NURTURE

HOW TO MAKE CARE YOUR COMPETITIVE ADVANTAGE

JANE ANDERSON

ABOUT THE AUTHOR

Jane Anderson is a strategic communications expert and is passionate about working with women in consulting. She has over 20 years' experience in corporate communications and capabilities, and she has worked with over 100,000 people to elevate their influence in their businesses and careers.

Jane has recently been voted as one of the top three branding gurus globally. She has won more than 25 marketing, sales and communication awards and also has one of the top 1% most viewed LinkedIn profiles.

She is the host of the iTunes podcast *The Jane Anderson Show*, and has achieved acclaim interviewing thought leaders and experts such as Seth Godin. Jane has also been featured in *Business Insider*, *Sky Business*, the *Sydney Morning Herald* and *The Age*, and she is a contributor on *Forbes*.

Her clients include some of the world's leading experts in their field, as well as iconic brands such as Virgin Australia, Lego, Ikea, Rio Tinto and Origin Energy.

Jane is also dedicated to helping female consultants position and promote themselves, and ensure that they're charging what they're worth. She has built (and continues to build) a diverse group of like-minded female industry leaders who support and help each other grow their practices.

Obsessed with elevating influence in all areas, Jane is the author of nine books, speaks at conferences and delivers group and one-on-one mentoring to consultants looking to grow their practices. She lives in Brisbane, Australia with her husband Mark and stubborn English Bulldog, Winston.

ACKNOWLEDGEMENT

At school I had an amazing business studies teacher called Mr Benfield. In fact, he was exceptional. He was kind, creative and quirky. I'm not a very competitive person but he seemed to bring out this side in me – one that I didn't even know I had. His teaching motivated and inspired me.

What made him unique was that he was a hippie. This was in a small country town in northern NSW, so it wasn't a big deal at all. But to have a hippie for a *business* teacher was pretty unique.

There was something else that made him better than other teachers – he used to set me reading assignments so that I could work ahead. I loved the subject, and when he saw that, he found expansion work for me to read in the textbook. On one occasion he even set me the task of teaching a lesson on vertical and horizontal integration to the entire class.

Mr Benfield knew how to cultivate my interest and get the most out of me. No other teacher that I had ever experienced was able to make a subject interesting enough to inspire me.

It became my best subject at school and, as a result, I decided to study business at university. I wanted to become a business studies teacher myself. Ultimately, I became a business coach instead of a teacher, but it was Mr Blenfield who helped me to realise what I loved and inspired me to follow a career in this space.

I've been fortunate to have some exceptional people in my life along with Mr Benfield who have inspired this book.

I will always be indebted to Matt Church for harnessing my thinking.

To the masters of their craft and my masterminds – Rowdy McLean, Keith Abraham, Amanda Stevens, Andrew Griffiths, Emma McQueen and Belinda Brosnan who have had such an impact on every idea in this book and pushed me far beyond what I could have achieved on my own. This would not have happened without you.

To the clients that I work with every day and who work on every aspect of this book in their practices – you are such an inspiration with the ripple you create in the world. I am grateful to see the work behind the scenes and admire how you constantly grapple with your ideas, messaging and positioning in order to make a difference on the planet.

To the team closest to me who make projects like this come to life. My husband Mark, who is one of the smartest and kindest human beings on the planet. His support along with my family has been unconditional. The late night proofreading and listening ear has been beyond invaluable. Thank you for your patience and making this come to life.

To my support team in the office, MC and Monique, who share the vision to create change, educate, innovate and help people grow their practices so they can have a greater impact in the world. Thank you for your hard work and looking after everything else so that I can get books like this completed!

Finally to my editor, Kristen Lowrey, and publisher, Sylvie Blair at BookPOD. Thank you for your commitment and dedication and being part of the team for every book project to date. Without you these ideas don't see the light of day.

Jane

CONTENTS

About the author v
Acknowledgement vi
Foreword x
Chapter 1: Why Care Matters 1
Chapter 2: What Holds Us Back From Making Care a Competitive Advantage 23
Chapter 3: Making Care Your Competitive Advantage 34
Chapter 4: Embracing Self-Care 43
Chapter 5: Customer Care 84
Chapter 6: Team Care 132
Chapter 7: In Closing 169
Work with Jane 171
Other titles by Jane Anderson 172

FOREWORD

What's your superpower in business and life?

I'm still discovering mine. But I know without a doubt that Jane Anderson's superpower is Nurture. Let me tell you why.

The first time Jane and I met, she had just delivered a speech on personal branding and was busy packing up while fielding fans. I wanted to approach her with a question I'd been too shy to raise in front of the large room, but she looked distracted, so I was hovering in the corner hoping she might notice me.

Likely picking up on the fact that I was behaving more like an awkward teenager than an aspiring businesswoman, Jane did notice me. She waved me over, and despite the buzzing room and other priorities, generously spent five minutes speaking with me.

Nurture is defined as caring for and protecting someone or something while they are growing. I've met many leaders who care, fewer who protect, and it's a rare gem like Jane who achieves both. Nurture truly is her superpower.

In those five minutes with me, Jane created an experience where I felt seen, supported, heard, and valued. I left our interaction with far more than an answer to my question: I left with new clarity and courage, plus a determination to offer others the same patience and care that Jane had shown me. And Jane left our interaction – perhaps unknowingly – with my loyalty and followship.

Through one act of nurture, lasting a matter of minutes, Jane gained commercial advantage. In the years since that first meeting, I have actively referred her to my clients, promoted her to my network, and bought her services myself. Yet beyond the commercial advantage lies a parallel gain in impact.

Jane's attention and generosity that day was a commercial turning point for me: following our conversation, I added six figures to my business revenue within six months. More meaningfully, it was a personal turning point: I added confidence and conviction to my career aspirations, without which I would not have grown my business so effectively. The impact Jane had on me, my business, and indirectly on my clients, is immeasurable. And it started with one small act of nurture.

With this book, Jane has gifted us all with a guide to finding and fostering nurture at work, and in doing so has placed in your hands a means to elevate both your commercial advantage and your leadership impact. She has unpacked what appears for her an intuitive practice of nurturing others, into an accessible framework so that we can all understand now to leverage nurture.

As you'll learn from these pages, care is no longer a leadership choice. It's a commercial expectation. Jane's timely and compelling description of how the world of work has fundamentally changed, and the necessity to now embed care and protection into our work, will help you embrace nurture and elevate your influence.

Nearly ten years after meeting Jane, I sought a coach to support me in establishing a new business. I chose Jane. Someone asked me, why her? My answer: because I needed someone who would nurture me, not just my business.

In our very first interaction, Jane demonstrated to me the importance of nurture to both my business and personal success. I did not forget this lesson. And now, with this book, perhaps I can turn nurture into my own superpower. Maybe you will, too.

Dr Kelly Windle
November 2023

CHAPTER 1

WHY CARE MATTERS

Introduction

On 18 March 2023, Julia Buckley praised British Airways in a viral tweet that has since gathered over 94,000 views.[1] In her comments, she commended the airline, and in particular the pilot, Captain Del, for single handedly 'curing 80% of [her] fear of flying'.

When Julia was boarding her British Airways flight she was incredibly nervous. But Captain Del – the pilot on that flight – came to her aid. He managed to allay her fears by taking the time to talk to her. He explained, and even drew, the aerodynamics that keep an airplane in the air.

The time that he spent with her – and, of course, his expertise – meant that Julia was able to feel confident in both the plane's design for flight, and in the flight crew themselves. And this confidence was truly 'life changing' for her.

---

1 Buckley, Julia (@juliathelast). 'For once i come to praise @British_Airways not to bury them. Boarded the 249 yday trembling with fear, disembarked serene w a diagram of aerodynamics drawn by pilot Del who singlehandedly cured 80% of my fear of flying. Potentially lifechanging. Thank you (+ Kai + Derek onboard).' 18 Mar 2023, 10.40pm. Tweet.

Captain Del likely had other things to do to prepare for his flight. But he didn't just hustle Julia along, or palm her off to a host. Instead, he spent the time and gave her the care that she needed to feel safe and confident on his plane.

Another story that I love is about a Spectrum Internet employee named Robert. He came to set up internet and streaming for a tired and stressed mama called Jessica. Jessica has two children including a son, Sailor, who was born blind and with two rare brain disorders. When Robert walked into Jessica's home, Sailor hadn't slept the night before and was inconsolable, and Jessica was overwhelmed trying to get everything done and care for two toddlers.

When Sailor walked up to Robert and reached up to be picked up, Robert didn't bat an eye. He just picked him up and cuddled him while he did his job. Jessica was so touched, she wrote a letter to the company saying:

'When Robert walked in and started talking, Sailor ran to him and reached up. Robert didn't seem bothered at all and, instead, held my son off and on for the whole 45 minutes he was in our home. He snuggled him close while I folded laundry. It was a huge relief to this tired momma. Robert could have walked in, rushed, and left but instead he saw a need greater than internet and met it. That's beyond customer service – it's humanity at its best. Robert deserves a raise… a promotion… something! He's an asset to your company and I will never forget his kindness. Sincerely, Jessica.'

What do these two stories have in common? They're both about the power of care.

I have also seen the power of care firsthand in my own business. A few years ago I was approached by John, a productivity expert who wanted to increase his practice from $800,000 a year to $1.5 million. He was very good at what he did and offered excellent programmes that brought fantastic results and outcomes for his clients. He did a great job at setting up all his systems and processes, was really good at connecting on LinkedIn and even better at getting people into his database. But he was struggling to get more traction in his business generally.

We sat down together to look at what he could do to grow his business and achieve the outcomes he wanted, and one of the first things we did was take a look at his database. John had a great database with over 7,400 people on it and lots of data about who bought from him, when and where.

I asked him to identify the people that had bought from him in the past that he loved working with. And when he did that, he came up with 40 individuals. But when I asked him the last time he had been in touch with those 40 people, it was on the last day that he delivered his programme. He hadn't reached out to a single customer since – and for some of them as much as 10 years had passed.

So then I asked him what he knew about each of these people. For most he could tell me their organisation and for some their role, but he didn't know any other details about them as individuals. Then I asked him if he'd ever taken them to lunch or organised thank you gifts or cards? But the answer was also no. It turned out that he didn't really know the people he was working for – not even his best customers.

John's downfall was not that he was a bad guy. He was actually a genuinely nice person. His downfall was that he tended to see everybody as a transaction.

For a productivity expert this approach makes sense. He did his job – excellently and efficiently – and when he was done he moved on to his next job. From his perspective this was the way to best deliver his expertise and grow his business... and he wasn't able to quantify the ROI on care and connection – on 'nurturing' his clients.

In my career, however, I've seen first hand the incredible return – in fact the 'competitive advantage' – you get from demonstrating care to your clients – as well as to your team and even yourself. And I knew that if we could incorporate those elements into his business, he would be able to grab that advantage for his own business.

So I challenged John to start reaching out to those 40 clients we had identified, and as a first step I suggested he put on a drinks event after work. I remember so clearly when I made the suggestion he kind of looked at me blankly and then he finally said, 'How do I do that?' I said, 'Well, you call the bar and make a booking, you call your clients and invite them and then you put a tab down.'

And to his credit that's just what he did. And then he kept reaching out. Again and again. The results? He doubled his revenue in the next 12 months. All because he implemented care – what I like to think of as 'nurture' – into his business approach.

It's important to note that this approach wasn't at all natural for John. But to his credit he took my message on board and made significant changes to how he interacted with his clients and the focus he put on relationship building. And that resulted in a huge difference in his business.

You don't have to be a natural extrovert, or someone who loves to organise events or meet up with people. You just have to care enough about the work you're doing and the people you're doing it for, to be proactive in maintaining your relationships with them. And that will lead to you better helping them to achieve their goals too.

The Nurture Value Model

John, Captain Del and Robert are all excellent examples of how practicing care and nurture in your business can help it thrive. But when we talk about care as a competitive advantage, what do we mean? Well, what we mean is that when you nurture and care for your clients you will experience increased retention, loyalty and sustainability in your business. In fact, that's really what this book is all about. Increasing the success and sustainability of your business through nurturing your relationships.

But before you can start the practice of nurture (the 'how' if you will), we need to understand where we are now and what's going on in the world. Importantly, we also need to get some insights into the ideal state of nurturing.

The Nurture Value Model

	Activity	Growth	Retention
5	Care	Growth	10 X
4	Prioritisation	Belonging	5X
3	Attention	Time	2X
2	Mindfulness	Community	0
1	Careless	Awareness	-1X

The Nurture Value Model is valuable to our understanding of nurture in business. It describes how we need to transform our culture of care in our businesses to drive up our retention of both clients and our team members, and create a more sustainable business.

At each level we have our activity and our focus and where these intersect we see the results on retention in our business. At each level, our activity becomes more aligned to care, our focus becomes more intensely on nurture and the impacts on our ability to retain clients and staff grows.

Level 1

So, at the lowest level – one – we are fairly careless in the activities that provide 'care' to the people we serve and work with (and even to ourselves). In the vast majority of cases it's simply because we're unaware that care needs to be part of our business focus. But while we might be unaware, the consequences are very real, and we can see a negative impact on our ability to retain those people important to our business success.

Level 2

At the second level, we've become more mindful of the nurture needed for our clients and team. We're focused on building or developing our community – whether in person or via social media or other networks. And because of this we're beginning to see a sort of parity in our retention.

At this level, we aren't losing clients or team members due to a lack of care, but we're not thriving either.

Level 3

At this third level, we've begun to give care more attention. And because of that, we're also giving it more time. It's become part of our team huddles, our mission and values and, even starting to be included in our systems. While we still have a ways to go, the result at this level is that we're able to increase our ability to retain good staff and clients by two times the previous level.

However, care hasn't taken enough of a prime position in our business or practice yet. We need to do more.

Level 4

At level four, we've taken our attention to care and turned it into a priority. Because of this, we're no longer focused just on our community, and we're doing more than just giving our focus on nurture some time – we're actually focused on creating a culture of belonging through our care of others.

This has an incredible impact, creating up to five times the retention rate with our teams and our clients.

Level 5

At this fifth and highest level we're giving both the most to nurturing our relationships, and getting the most return in the form of retention. Here care isn't just a priority, it's a systematic element of our business or practice. It is infused in every aspect of the work that we do. And in delivering it we're focused on growth – that's both the growth and development of the members of our team, as well as growing our business or practice and helping our clients to grow and develop within their own businesses as we support them.

The result is that we're able to build the processes, systems and mindset right into our work, creating maximum retention of clients and team, even up to 10 times what we might otherwise be able to do.

It is here that our transformation to making care our competitive advantage is complete. We've positioned ourselves to be able to nurture our clients, our team and even ourselves in the best, but also most efficient and effective way possible. Because of this, we are able to embrace care into every aspect of our work, and truly make a difference in retention – and therefore the sustainability and success of our business and practice.

Care: Why It Matters

Why does care create such an impact in our work? Why does this seemingly simple change in outlook (and practice) create such a dramatic change in our business retention and success? It all comes down to what's going on in the world, in the economy and with the people that we want to both help and work with.

So let's dive into why care matters.

It's always mattered

In reality, the ability to nurture your team and clients has always mattered because wellbeing (and retention and sustainability) has always mattered. But it hasn't always been *valued*.

Today, things are slowly changing. There is a much better understanding about the importance of the wellbeing of people, relationships and even organisations as an entity, and it's become a vital part of a business strategy.[2] Researchers call this 'strategic caring' and research shows that when you care for the people within and around your business, they will care for and be loyal to your business in return.[3]

A team, for example, that feels they are 'thriving' is 200% better at adapting to change, 41% less likely to miss work and 81% less likely to look for a new employer.[4] They're also more resilient and engaged.[5] And all of that means that caring for your team is more than a 'nice to have' but a true competitive advantage in your business.[6]

---

[2] Jacoby, A. (21 September 2022). 'Three Steps To Making A Culture Of Well-Being A Strategic Priority'. *Forbes*. Available at https://www.forbes.com/sites/forbescoachescouncil/2022/09/21/three-steps-to-making-a-culture-of-well-being-a-strategic-priority/?sh=275bd51e3ca6.

[3] Gabsa, R and Rastogi, S. (23 June 2020). 'Take Care of Your People, and They'll Take Care of Business'. Gallup: Workplace. Available at https://www.gallup.com/workplace/312824/care-people-care-business.aspx.

[4] Gabsa & Rastogi. 'Take Care of Your People, and They'll Take Care of Business'.

[5] Gabsa & Rastogi. 'Take Care of Your People, and They'll Take Care of Business'.

[6] Poškienė, E, Coudounaris, D and Kazlauskaite, R. (2020). The Relationship between Caring for Employees and the Well-being of the Organisation. *Management of Organizations: Systematic Research*. Available at https://www.researchgate.net/publication/342424944_The_Relationship_between_Caring_for_Employees_and_the_Well-being_of_the_Organisation_Management_of_Organizations_Systematic_Research_2020_Vol_84_pp45-60/citation/download.

In the same way, caring for your customers leads to better results for your business or practice. In fact, a 5% increase in customer satisfaction can lead to an increase in company revenue of up to 95%.[7]

We're experiencing rapid change

The level of change that people are experiencing is rapidly increasing. We're seeing massive innovation and disruption as we head into the digital age, and one of the top challenges that executives and experts are facing is one of 'digital disruption'.[8]

Consider the recent launch of ChatGPT, the AI innovations happening across the business world and the new tech that is being created every day, including tech that is changing the way that we fundamentally operate in the world. In fact, research by Goldman Sachs predicts that two-thirds of all our current occupations could be at least partially automated by AI and 46% of administrative jobs could be fully automated by AI in the future.[9]

We're also seeing an adjustment to the new 'world of work'. During COVID, people had to quickly adjust to working from home. But now CEOs across the globe are facing pressure to get teams back into the office – and many people are reluctant.[10] The debate rages on – leading

---

[7] Bernazzani, S. 'Here's Why Customer Retention is So Important for ROI, Customer Loyalty, and Growth'. Hubspot. Available at https://blog.hubspot.com/service/customer-retention.

[8] Khanna, R. (2022). Dignity in a Digital Age: Making Tech Work for All of Us. Simon & Schuster.

[9] Global Economics Analyst: The Potentially Large Effects of Artificial Intelligence on *Economic Growth*. (26 March 2023). [Report]. Goldman Sachs. Available at https://www.key4biz.it/wp-content/uploads/2023/03/Global-Economics-Analyst_-The-Potentially-Large-Effects-of-Artificial-Intelligence-on-Economic-Growth-Briggs_Kodnani.pdf.

[10] Tanzi, B & Boyle, M. (26 March 2023). 'Remote work gains momentum despite return-to-office mandates from high-profile CEOs'. *Fortune*. Available at

workers and teams to have more uncertainty into what their work life will look like in the future.

These factors have come together to create a level of change that means that a lot of people are spending an increasing amount of time and energy simply trying to keep up with all the changes. And at the individual level people are in overwhelm. They aren't coping under the pressure, and because they're stretched so thin, they're having to try to do more with less. If you're wondering if this is happening in your team and with your customers and clients, I can assure you that it is. In fact, you're most likely feeling this as well.

Equally, organisations are feeling the pressure to flexibly adapt to these widespread changes. They (and their leaders) are under pressure to find ways to support their staff with wellbeing programmes that give them help to manage and even thrive during change.

However, the problem that we're seeing is that these wellbeing programmes – where they are offered – are operating in isolation from leadership development. So rather than helping leaders to learn how to look after – or nurture – their teams, we're just teaching them how to deliver wellbeing programmes. And that's simply not enough.

In the same way, organisations, experts, thought leaders and business owners are all looking for better ways to support customers and clients who are also struggling to adapt to rapid change. They're looking for better systems and communications in order to bring better results for those that they help. And it's a struggle to meet those clients where they are in a time of upheaval and uncertainty.

---

https://fortune.com/2023/03/25/remote-work-gains-momentum-despite-return-to-office-mandates-from-high-profile-ceos/.

Future skills are changing

In the future, we're going to need new skills, different from ever before. This puts a lot of pressure on leaders, business owners and practitioners who need to keep their own skills, and the skills of their team, up to date.

In the future researchers and 'thinkers' predict that we'll need more ability to have virtual collaboration and cross cultural competency.[11] We'll also need to have more media literacy – particularly focused on the changing platforms of communication – and be comfortable working across disciplines.[12]

Finding these skills – or developing and growing them – is a task that leaders have to begin to undertake. And employees who are not being developed are going to look elsewhere for roles where they will be able to grow. Otherwise, they know they'll be left behind in our rapidly changing world of work.

We've seen the amplification of mental health issues

The pandemic saw the structures that supported care in the workplace crumble, leaving people on their own, and feeling lost and unsure. During this time, anxiety and depression in adults skyrocketed by a massive 25%.[13] People became more disconnected and isolated than

---

[11] Davies, A, Fidler, D & Gorbis, M. (2020). Future Work Skills 2020. [Report]. The University of Phoenix Research Institute. Available at https://www.iftf.org/projects/future-work-skills-2020/.

[12] Davies, A. Future Work Skills 2020. [Report].

[13] Czeisler, M.É. , Lane, R.I., Petrosky, E., et al. (2020). Mental Health, Substance Use, and Suicidal Ideation During the COVID-19 Pandemic — United States, June 24–30, 2020. *Morbidity and Mortality Weekly Report, 69(32),* 1049–1057. Available at https://www.cdc.gov/mmwr/volumes/69/wr/mm6932a1.htm?s_cid=mm6932a1_w and *COVID-19 pandemic triggers 25% increase in prevalence of anxiety and depression worldwide.* (2022). [News Release]. World Health Organization.

ever and loneliness vastly increased.[14] Individuals lost jobs – with both job loss and unemployment associated with adverse mental health outcomes.[15] Others had to learn to work remotely almost overnight, leaving them stressed and unmoored.[16]

It was also harder to get medical care, both physical and mental, and they were disconnected from their own leadership, which saw people struggling through this change on their own.

This impacts your team, of course. But it's important to understand that your client's are struggling with the same impacts. Even three years on, the effects of the pandemic continue with 90% of adults in the US believing that they're facing a mental health crisis, including increased isolation and loneliness, job loss and financial instability.[17] It's no better in Australia, with research showing that there have been significant

---

Available at https://www.who.int/news/item/02-03-2022-covid-19-pandemic-triggers-25-increase-in-prevalence-of-anxiety-and-depression-worldwide.

[14] Australian Institution of Health and Welfare. (2021). *Social isolation and loneliness.* Australian Government. Available at https://www.aihw.gov.au/reports/australias-welfare/social-isolation-and-loneliness-covid-pandemic.

[15] Reeves, A., McKee, M. and Stuckler, D. (2014). Economic suicides in the Great Recession in Europe and North America. *Br J Psychiatry, 205(3)*, 246-7. Available at https://pubmed.ncbi.nlm.nih.gov/24925987/.

[16] Xiao, Y., Becerik-Gerber, B., Lucas, G., and Roll, S.C. (2021). Impacts of Working From Home During COVID-19 Pandemic on Physical and Mental Well-Being of Office Workstation Users. *J Occup Environ Med, 63(3),* 181-190. Available at https://www.ncbi.nlm.nih.gov/pmc/articles/PMC7934324/.

[17] Panchal, N, Saunders, H & Rudowitz, R. (20 March 2023). 'The Implications of COVID-19 for Mental Health and Substance Use'. KFF. Available at https://www.kff.org/coronavirus-covid-19/issue-brief/the-implications-of-covid-19-for-mental-health-and-substance-use/.

increases in depression and anxiety continuing as compared to pre-pandemic levels.[18]

This is also something that you – as a business owner, consultant or thought leader needs to be aware of for yourself as well. Whether related to post-pandemic mental health issues, or not, we're also seeing a great deal more burn out. One fantastic example is Jacinda Ahern, the former New Zealand Prime Minister. Many believed she was at the top of her game when she announced her resignation from the role. The reason why – she just felt burnt out.[19]

She's not the only one. This is becoming an all-too common problem for people who are trying to cope with the upheavals of the last few years, as well as create a sustainable life for the future.

Leaders aren't trained to provide care for struggling staff

With staff suffering, leaders are finding it uncomfortable. They're not feeling confident to have wellbeing discussions with their team because they're simply not qualified. They don't know how to handle those discussions and they don't feel that they're in a position to provide advice or support. They also feel concerned they might handle it the wrong way, and do more harm than good.

This can lead to awkwardness in the conversations when they're approached by their staff. Or leaders might take an overly formal approach that leaves their staff feeling more isolated or even

---

[18] (9 March 2023). 'Moving on from COVID means facing its impact on mental health, say experts'. University of Sydney. Available at https://www.sydney.edu.au/news-opinion/news/2023/03/09/moving-on-from-covid-means-facing-its-impact-on-mental-health--s.html.

[19] Hjelmgaard, K. (19 January 2023). 'Not "enough in the tank": New Zealand prime minister Jacinda Ardern quits over burnout'. USA TODAY. Available at https://www.usatoday.com/story/news/world/2023/01/19/new-zealand-prime-minister-jacinda-ardern-resigns/11080726002/.

embarrassed. Or they may simply escalate the conversation to HR straight away[20], or even try to refer the staff member onto professional help, rather giving them the support they need in that moment.

In this case it isn't necessarily about a lack of care. It's more about a lack of confidence to provide the care that is necessary. But it's the care that matters.

People are leaving the workforce

From quiet quitting to the Great Resignation, nearly 40% of the workforce are currently considering leaving their employer within the next 12 months.[21] Retention is becoming more and more important, and care is one of the most important factors (in conjunction with rate of pay, naturally) when it comes to retaining top talent.[22]

However, research shows that employers aren't embracing the care factor enough. Nearly 50% of Australian employers have 'no intention' of updating their employee value proposition – the way they communicate the tangle and intangible rewards, opportunities and benefits that someone might get from working in their organisation – in an effort to attract and retain better and more talented employees.[23]

Yet we know that post-Covid people are more and more considering why they are working with any particular organisation and if they are really achieving their potential. And experts believe that now is the time to

---

[20] *How to support staff who are experiencing a mental health problem.* (n.d.). [Resource]. Mind. Available at https://www.mind.org.uk/media-a/4661/resource4.pdf.

[21] *What workers want: Winning the war for talent.* (n.d.). [Report]. PWC. Available at https://www.pwc.com.au/important-problems/future-of-work/what-workers-want-report.pdf.

[22] What workers want: Winning the war for talent. PWC.

[23] What workers want: Winning the war for talent. PWC.

double down on development efforts to allow opportunities for workers to continue to grow and develop based on their potential.[24]

If we aren't giving our staff reasons to stay with us, and the opportunities to develop and grow, then we are going to face increasing employee turnover and churn. People want to feel like they belong and like they matter.

On the other hand, when you take care of your employees they're more engaged and loyal. Engaged employees are more productive, collaborative and innovative.[25] You get increased productivity and innovation, higher workplace morale, more job satisfaction and more dedication as well.

Your clients and customers are facing this same dilemma as well. Whether they're working to keep their own team in place, or are struggling with decisions about their own future, it's a problem that is impacting much of Australia – and one we need to be aware of when providing care to our clients.

Organisations are struggling to meet their female leadership targets

Organisations today are struggling to meet their female leadership targets. In Australia today, only 19% of CEOs are female, and women make up less than a third of all key management positions across the

---

[24] Schwartz, J., Denny, B., and Mallon, D. (2020). *Returning to work in the future of work: Embracing purpose, potential, perspective, and possibility during COVID-19.* Deloitte. Available at https://www2.deloitte.com/us/en/insights/focus/human-capital-trends/2020/covid-19-and-the-future-of-work.html.

[25] Baldoni, J. (2013). Employee Engagement Does More than Boost Productivity. *Harvard Business Review*. Available at https://hbr.org/2013/07/employee-engagement-does-more.

nation.[26] But women are tired of accepting this gap. Women in general are demanding more opportunities at work, and women leaders are moving companies at a record rate. It's such a phenomenon in fact, that experts are referring to this as 'The Great Break Up'.[27]

The reasons that women are leaving organisations in unprecedented numbers essentially comes down to care. Research shows that women are seeing that they will struggle to advance from the subtle undercurrents of their leaders and the organisations. They often face microaggressions with people they work with questioning their decisions. And they're aware that while they might 'have a seat at the table' their voices are still not being heard.

To combat this lack of care, women that are actually in leadership positions are trying to do more, give more and care more (this may be you!). They're taking on more tasks to support wellbeing and inclusion within their organisations, but they aren't being appropriately compensated either with pay rate or with support to do those additional projects on top of their regular roles. This leaves them feeling underappreciated and stretched very thin. And they aren't seeing their need for flexibility, wellbeing and inclusion being taken seriously at the organisational level.[28]

---

[26] (8 March 2023). 'Gender targets miss the mark for women in leadership'. University of South Australia. Available at https://www.unisa.edu.au/media-centre/Releases/2023/gender-targets-miss-the-mark-for-women-in-leadership/.

[27] Krivkovich, A., Liu, W.W., Nguyen, H., et.al., (2022). *Women in the Workplace 2022*. [Report]. McKinsey & Company. Available at https://www.mckinsey.com/featured-insights/diversity-and-inclusion/women-in-the-workplace.

[28] Krivkovich, A., Liu, W.W., Nguyen, H., et.al., (2022).

Digitisation means more automation and less human contact than ever

Over the weekend I rang Westpac to solve a small problem I was having with my banking cards. Because it wasn't a 'typical problem' the automated customer service assistance system simply wasn't set up to help me. So I kept going round and round in circles trying to get the answer I was looking for. I kept getting sent to the website and onto banking services or the system would just hang up on me, forcing me to start the frustrating process all over again.

In order to get anywhere I eventually realised I had to actually *not* say what I wanted (because what I wanted simply confused the automated system). It was the only way to finally get through to an actual person who could assist me.

Westpac had implemented digitisation in an effort to improve customer service, but it had failed. Instead, I struggled to reach someone who could think outside of the box and help me solve my problem. Automation and digitisation took away the opportunity for the care that could come from human contact.

While digitisation can help us with bulk jobs and interactions, with its implementation we've lost the human touch. Today we spend a lot of time shopping online. Where previously you could go into a store and people would recognise you and give you support and suggestions, now we go onto a website and an algorithm identifies what we might like and showcases that for us. We've lost the ability to interact and gain more information and insight this way. And that is a problem for our own customers and clients who don't want to feel like a number, or worse, a dollar sign.

Evidence suggests that customers prefer to engage with humans rather than AI when it comes to customer service.[29] Research also shows that customers and clients are more willing to engage with an organisation and are more likely to reach a conclusion they're satisfied with when they are dealing with humans.[30]

That is because a human provides a care factor that automation simply can't. And while automating customer service can get you so far, there's a natural limit to its effectiveness in actually providing customer care. Because that is about relationships. And you simply can't have a relationship with a computer or software solution.

In the same way, today many business owners and practitioners are too reliant on 'tools' to organise their teams. While I'm a huge advocate for systems and tools, and the efficiencies these can bring, they must be backed up with face-to-face meetings, daily huddles and other opportunities for connection, training, feedback and mentoring.

Without these opportunities for human interaction – and for the care that comes from that human interaction – your team can start to feel like just another cog in the wheel. They can lose engagement and purpose, and when that happens, they'll start to look for a role where they might get more opportunities for growth and development.

We're spending too much time on social media platforms

Tracey is a coach in my community who spends a great deal of time online both with her work and personal life. While she's on those

---

[29] Gao, Y., Rui, H., and Sun, S. (2021). The Value of Humanization in Customer Service. [Conference paper]. *54th Hawaii International Conference on System Sciences*, Maui, USA. Available at https://scholarspace.manoa.hawaii.edu/server/api/core/bitstreams/7d2659eb-2304-40be-80a0-c9f363183989/content.

[30] Gao, Y., Rui, H., and Sun, S. (2021).

platforms she's working with her own coaching community, and talking, writing and even reading about coaching. So the algorithms on those platforms are naturally seeing that attention and serving her up more and more ads and posts from other coaches and coaching programs and the like.

Because of this onslaught of focused information Tracey has the perception that the coaching world is becoming more and more cutthroat with more competition and less opportunities. But that's not *actually* the case. It's only the case because she is seeing everything that social media can serve up in the coaching space. And that is only happening because she's spending too much time working and hanging out in the digital world and not enough time in the real world.

Because of the way it's been developed, social media gives you a skewed perception about what is happening in the world. And while many people believe that they 'must' have a social media presence if they want to have a successful business or practice, that's not actually the case. In fact, I have 12 clients that are not even on social media and have highly successful businesses.

Social media has also changed how we connect with each other and, importantly, how we connect with our customers and clients. Social media makes it easier to reach out to customers. It's so easy in fact, that we often use this as our primary means of communication.

But when we interact solely on social media we lose that vital personal human connection. And that's primarily because it's a broadcast connection. Unless you're directly messaging a customer, and sometimes even then, they won't know if it's you that is really responding to them, or if it's someone who works for you or even a bot. And when you do use those automations, it's like outsourcing your care. It's OK to do it occasionally. But it certainly won't develop your relationships with your clients and customers.

It costs more to acquire new customers than retain them

If you're in business you're likely aware that acquiring a new customer costs you five times more (or even up to 25 times more![31]) than simply retaining the customers you already have. Because of that, if you're able to retain just 5% more customers, you can see your profits increase by a minimum of 25% and by as much as 95%.[32]

Even more, when it comes to selling new products or services to customers, existing customers will buy from you up to 70% of the time. But with a new customer your success rate is only 5-20%.[33]

It just makes good financial sense to nurture the clients that you have now.

You get a better ROI

Put simply, when you nurture your customers, you'll see a fantastic return on your investment. Good customer care leads to good customer relationships, taking one-time clients and turning them into long-term brand champions[34].

This is important because when a customer or client has a good experience with you or from you, they're more likely to buy from you

---

[31] *What is Conversion Rate Optimization? 7 Minute Guide From Beginner to Advanced.* (2019). Invesp. Available at https://www.invespcro.com/blog/customer-acquisition-retention/.

[32] Reichheld, F. (n.d.). *Prescription for Cutting Costs.* Bain & Company. Available at https://media.bain.com/Images/BB_Prescription_cutting_costs.pdf.

[33] Landis, T. (2022). *Customer Retention Marketing vs. Customer Acquisition Marketing.* Elm Street Outbound Engine. Available at https://www.outboundengine.com/blog/customer-retention-marketing-vs-customer-acquisition-marketing/.

[34] *Must-know customer service statistics of 2023 (so far).* (2023). Khoros. Available at https://khoros.com/blog/must-know-customer-service-statistics.

again.[35] In fact, 93% of customers will make another purchase when they've received excellent customer care in the past.[36] And 78% will still make another purchase even if a company has made a mistake as long as the customer care is excellent.[37]

On the other hand, without customer care your brand will suffer. Research shows that well over half of people will change brands or service providers if they don't receive the customer care they expect.[38] Only 15% of customers will forgive a single bad experience when they consider the brand to provide bad customer care generally.[39] As opposed to 80% who would forgive a bad single bad experience as long as they generally receive excellent customer care.[40]

Taking care of yourself increases productivity and innovation

Care in your business isn't solely focused on others. In fact, when you focus on your own physical, mental and emotional wellbeing first, you'll be more productive and have greater innovation within your business.

---

[35] *State of the Connected Customer – 4th Edition.* (2020). [Report]. Salesforce. Available at https://www.salesforce.com/content/dam/web/it_it/www/pdf/connected-customer-report-2020.pdf.

[36] Redbord, M. (2022). *The Hard Truth About Acquisition Costs (and How Your Customers Can Save You).* Hubspot. Available at https://blog.hubspot.com/service/customer-acquisition-study?.

[37] State of the Connected Customer – 4th Edition. (2020). Salesforce.

[38] Must-know customer service statistics of 2023 (so far). (2023). Khoros.

[39] Dorsey, M., Segall, D., and Temkin, B. (2019). *ROI of Customer Experience.* [Report]. Qualtrics XM Institute. Available at https://www.qualtrics.com/m/assets/wp-content/uploads/2019/12/XMI_ROIofCustomerExperience-2019.pdf

[40] Dorsey, Segall and Temkin. (2019).

Stress is a business killer. It leads to physical problems – such as headaches[41] and loss of sleep[42]. And it contributes to long-term diseases such as heart disease and high blood pressure[43]. It also slows you down mentally and reduces your focus and motivation and it has even been linked to a higher risk of Alzheimer's and dementia[44].

Taking care of yourself combats these problems leaving you with more clarity, more health and more mental wellbeing to tackle the rigours of your business day in and day out.

So Why Aren't We Focused More On Care?

It seems pretty clear that care is an important part of any business or practice. But why aren't we focussing on it more? What holds us back? Let's find out.

---

[41] (9 August 2022). 'Headaches: Reduce stress to prevent the pain'. Mayo Clinic. Available at https://www.mayoclinic.org/diseases-conditions/tension-headache/in-depth/headaches/art-20046707#:~:text=It's%20not%20a%20coincidence%20%E2%80%94%20headaches,in%20children%20and%20young%20adults.

[42] Johnson, J. (5 September 2018). 'How to tell if stress is affecting your sleep'. *Medical News Today*. Available at https://www.medicalnewstoday.com/articles/322994#takeaway.

[43] 'Stress Can Increase Your Risk for Heart Disease'. University of Rochester Medical Center, Health Encyclopedia. Available at https://www.urmc.rochester.edu/encyclopedia/content.aspx?ContentTypeID=1&ContentID=2171#:~:text=Studies%20suggest%20that%20the%20high,plaque%20deposits%20in%20the%20arteries.

[44] (15 February 2021). 'Protect your brain from stress'. Harvard Health Publishing: Harvard Medical School. Available at https://www.health.harvard.edu/mind-and-mood/protect-your-brain-from-stress.

CHAPTER 2

WHAT HOLDS US BACK FROM MAKING CARE A COMPETITIVE ADVANTAGE

We know that nurturing ourselves, our clients and our staff matters. We've explored many of the reasons why. But even when we understand the importance of nurture and care, we sometimes struggle to implement it into our practices and businesses. And that's because there are things that hold us back from nurturing our clients and staff, even if we don't realise it.

So what are some of those things that hold us back from not only making care an integral part of our practices and businesses, but also for harnessing it as a competitive advantage?

What Holds Us Back From Making Care a Competitive Advantage

We believe we are too busy

The belief that we are too busy is one of the main reasons why we don't nurture ourselves, our clients or our staff in our practices. And you likely are very busy running your business as well as managing your personal and home lives. But what if many of the things that make us feel 'busy' could be better managed to create more productivity with less effort?

When I worked as a productivity expert for the world's largest productivity consulting company, I found that people spent a great deal of time on activities that simply weren't impactful or didn't give them a great return. In fact, in a survey conducted by Zapier, 83% of workers said they spent one to three hours a day 'covering for or making up work for a colleague'.[1] This is in line with my own experience, where I found that 50–60% of an employee's time is actually spent helping someone else out or answering questions posed to them.

But nurturing others – or having 'a culture of care' – is actually a great way to bring those numbers down. Here's how.

Imagine that Beryl works on the finance team in your office, but she doesn't understand how to run a report that is part of her job. So, every time she needs that report, she comes to you for help.

You want to be helpful, but you're also really busy, so you quickly run those reports for Beryl yourself. After all, it only takes you five minutes and it's much quicker if you get it done yourself. But that is five minutes of your day that you lose, every time that she needs that report. And while you're being *helpful* you aren't actually nurturing Beryl and you're contributing to your overall sense of 'busy-ness'.

On the other hand, when you are focused on *nurturing*, you won't just spend five minutes helping Beryl. You'll actually take the time to stop and teach her how to run the report herself. This might take a little longer on the front end – maybe even an hour or two. But taking the time now will scrape back all those minutes over the next year that you would have been distracted from your own work. Your investment in

---

[1] *Meetings aren't killing productivity; data entry is* (2021). Zapier. Available at https://zapier.com/blog/report-how-office-workers-spend-time/.

nurturing Beryl means you get a return on your time and she gets the opportunity for growth and development. A win-win.

As another example, imagine you're an expert who has a client who calls every week for advice on how to manage a task. Rather than fielding that call each week and helping them out, which is likely your first reaction, you could instead consider what kind of system you might be able to put into place to help and nurture your client.

Maybe you have a staff member who can jump in and pre-empt this particular problem. Or maybe you spend some time helping them set up an internal system that can help. Or maybe you need to offer your client some additional training or advice that can help them in the future. Whatever the system is, this will allow you to help them while saving your time in the future.

At the end of the day, busy-ness is a real problem when it comes to nurturing your clients and staff. But, as we've touched on here and we'll continue to show you in the rest of this book, nurturing is actually one way to give yourself back a great deal of time and even energy in the long run.

We fear it will impact our ability to run the business

I have a friend who is very caring. In fact, she is so caring that she often becomes embroiled in the dramas of others, including her clients. This has become a problem because the dramas are overtaking her ability to actually provide the services (which she's fantastic at) to those very same clients.

It's not just the amount of time it's taking from her business. It's the fact that those clients are coming to her and focusing on those dramas rather than focusing on the work that needs to be done in their own businesses. And while their dramas are dragging themselves down, my client is allowing herself to be dragged down as well.

In the same way, we worry about becoming 'embroiled' in the drama or the lives of our staff if we 'care' too much. This might cause us to shy away from getting to know our staff well. And it can also cause us to ignore, or at least downplay, drama that might be occurring between our staff members. However, we can't ignore workplace drama which can decrease productivity, increase anxiety and tension and result in staff leaving (the opposite of our retention goals!).

While it is a valid fear – that becoming 'too close' to or caring too much about our clients or staff can impact our ability to run our business – the actual problem is in not caring in the right way. At the end of the day, *nurture* is not the same as entanglement. And just because you focus on nurturing your clients and staff, doesn't mean that you need to become entangled in their day-to-day dramas (in fact, in most cases, you shouldn't!).

Nurturing can't be at the expense of your ability to run your business. Most business owners, experts and thought leaders recognise this fact quite clearly. And it's precisely this fear – among other worries – that hold us back from nurturing clients, staff, ourselves and others in our practices.

But understanding *how* to provide care and nurturing to your clients and staff is the most important part of helping you to move past this fear. Because understanding how to do it will allow you to care and nurture your clients and staff without impacting your business negatively. In fact, it will have a positive impact on your business!

We don't want to 'baby' others

Another thing that holds us back from nurturing others is a fear that if we 'help' too much we might be seen as babying others – particularly our staff. In other words, we might appear that we aren't empowering others to take on their own development and growth. We might even think things like, 'I had to do this, why shouldn't they?' or 'They're only going to learn if they try for themselves.'

The problem is that where we are today is much different to where we were five, 10 or 15 years ago. Today there is a greater volume of work, more content, increased data, drastically more available information and so on. And the speed of change in the workplace reflects that. Today, people simply need more help than you think because of this speed of change.

That doesn't mean that you shouldn't empower them. Giving your staff training, opportunities and experience to develop and grow is vital. This allows them to stand on their own two feet (after a time). To nurture clients, you need to give them insight, transparency and education so they can feel empowered working with you.

However, in order to do this well, you need to recognise where you are on the nurturing spectrum. Imagine that one end of the spectrum is complete autonomy – in other words, assuming your clients and staff will just 'figure it out'. Then on the other side of the spectrum is 'babying' your clients and staff – or assuming they won't or can't understand and doing everything for them.

When it comes to nurturing well, you have to understand where you and your clients are on the spectrum. When you're passing on opportunities or tasks to your staff, or when you're providing advice or feedback to your clients, are you assuming too much? Does your client or team member need more support before moving towards a resolution or solution? Are you smothering them or assuming they know less than they do?

It all comes down to providing the support they need in a way that allows them to learn, grow and develop. You can think of this kind of support like a plant. While the plant is young, it needs more water. But once it gets older and its roots are deeper and longer, then it needs water less often, because it can access water from deep in the soil itself.

In the same way, your clients and staff need more help in the beginning of your relationship or any new project or task. But as you provide that and they grow their own roots, they'll need less from you.

As business author and speaker Tom Peters says: 'Management is about arranging and telling. Leadership is about nurturing and enhancing.'

We worry we will be seen as a 'rescuer'

The fear of becoming a 'rescuer' is another reason why we may not initially focus on nurturing our clients or staff. The idea of a rescuer was set out in research by Stephen B. Karpman, M.D.[2]

Karpman's Drama Triangle

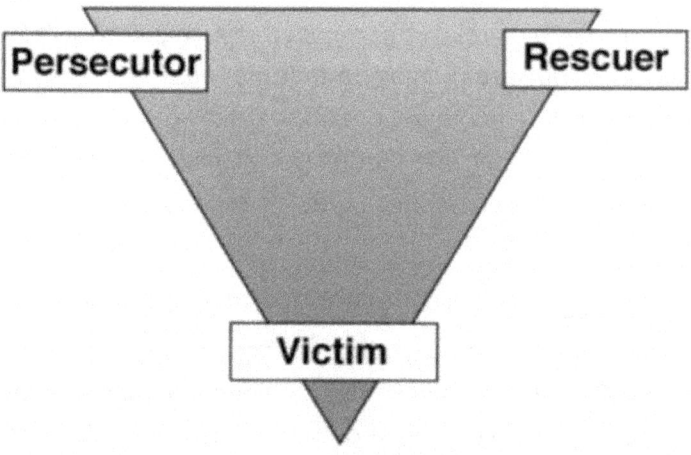

Karpman's Drama Triangle is a dynamic model of social interaction and conflict, which posits that people often play the unconscious roles of victim, persecutor or rescuer. The victim is the person who says, 'Poor

---

[2] Karpman, S. Karpman Drama Triangle. Available at https://karpmandramatriangle.com/.

me.' The persecutor is the person who is criticising or blaming the victim. And the rescuer is the person who says, 'Let me help you!'

Interestingly, not every person in this triangle will always realise what role they are playing. Someone – an employer, for example – can be cast in the role of persecutor without even knowing. People are often drawn into the triangle against their wishes or are forced to play roles that may not even relate to the actual circumstances.

It's important that those drawn into the triangle work to remove themselves. Otherwise they can find themselves tugged into a situation that they don't want to be in, playing a role they don't want to play or, even worse, seen to be playing into the drama.

As employers, however, we can often be concerned about being seen as a rescuer. This is because being a rescuer – particularly when this is an ongoing role that you've been cast in (or cast yourself in) – can take a lot of time out of your business. When you're a rescuer you can create a dysfunctional dynamic that creates a dependency on you. This can feel good for a while, but the dependency feeds itself and your staff will become more and more reliant on you which can take up more and more time. It also undermines their ability to become empowered and solve their own problems.

However, it's not always as easy as simply removing yourself from the situation – particularly when you've found yourself in the role of the rescuer. And that's because being a rescuer is often driven by a desire to be 'contributing' or 'helping'. So while we worry that we'll be seen as a rescuer, we may struggle to stop actually doing the things that make us a rescuer. And that can lead to its own problems in your business or practice.

It's important to recognise that 'rescuing' is not the same as nurturing. While both involve an element of helping, a rescuer isn't offering authentic or altruistic help. They aren't trying to help the other person (staff or client!) to grow or develop. Instead, the rescuer's help only encourages the other person to continue to depend on the helper.

On the other hand, when you nurture someone you are helping them to grow and develop and seize opportunities that are for their benefit now and in the long run. This *will* lead to empowering them to take actions that will not lead to them depending more on you, but depending less (in the best ways).

We worry we'll be seen as self-absorbed

Sometimes the person that we need to nurture is ourselves – yes, even within our businesses and practices. We'll talk more about the importance of self-care later in the book but suffice it to say that this is a very important element of nurture in general, because without self-care (or better yet, self-nurture) we simply won't have enough in the tank to nurture others.

But when it comes to self-nurture, many of us struggle, particularly within our businesses. And often that's because we don't want to seem self-absorbed.

It can feel unnatural to focus on ourselves, and doubly so when we actually have to carve out time or resources to do so. For example, many business owners would feel guilty to assign their team members a project to work on and then duck out for a Pilates class, or for a lunchtime walk. Or they may feel uncomfortable spending money to get personal support – whether that's childcare or a housecleaner – just so they can spend more time on their business. But at the end of the day, supporting yourself is supporting your business.

Another way that this fear can play out is when we set boundaries between our personal and work lives. So often I hear from people in my community that they struggle to say 'no'. I understand this. As someone who wants to nurture and care for my clients and staff it can be difficult to set boundaries. But if we don't – if we aren't able to set appropriate boundaries – then we won't have the energy or resources to properly nurture our clients and staff anyway.

It also feels scary to say no because of the fear that you might stop the flow of work coming into your business. After all, if you turn down this project, who knows when the next one might appear? But saying no – or setting boundaries – can actually be beneficial to your business. It allows you to provide your clients with a better quality of work. It helps you to demonstrate to your clients where your boundaries are – which they will learn to respect in the future. For example, if you always say no to weekend work, they'll soon learn to reach out during the regular working week if they want to work with you. And it can also help you to leave time and space for better work in the future. If you're already working at capacity, what will you do when that dream project lands on your doorstep?

It's only by nurturing yourself, setting those boundaries and letting go of the fear of looking self-absorbed by doing so, that you can truly begin nurturing others.

We're afraid we don't know how to help

When it comes to nurturing our clients and staff (and even ourselves) sometimes the fear that holds us back is simply a fear that we don't know how to really care for our clients. For some of us, the typical way that we see 'caring' portrayed just doesn't come naturally. This is a lot like my client John from the last chapter.

Maybe you're more introverted. Maybe you're just the type of personality that is more naturally focused on numbers and results, rather than relationships. Maybe you have a lot of personal demands that make it tricky to focus on others outside of your immediate family. Or maybe – and particularly when it comes to your staff – you worry that you don't know how to truly nurture someone.

This is certainly a valid fear and one that many leaders and business owners face. We want to help others grow and develop but we undervalue our own skills and abilities to help make that happen. That's where this book comes in. In the next few chapters we'll help you to step from understanding the value of nurturing others in your business, to understanding *how* to do just that.

Are you holding back from nurturing your clients or staff?

At this stage you might be wondering if you are holding yourself back from really nurturing your clients or staff. You can check in with yourself by asking yourself the following questions:

1. Do your staff believe they're achieving their potential? If not, how can you help them?

2. Are your clients able to get the support they need from you without impacting your own productivity? If not, what systems and structures can you put in place to start nurturing clients while maintaining your own boundaries?

3. Are you able to set the boundaries and support yourself in a way that will allow you to create a sustainable business? If not, what could you do to help you make that change?

Conclusion

Understanding the fears and worries that hold us back from caring and nurturing others is a vital part of implementing the elements that you need to create a culture of care in your business. Once you understand your own unique challenges, you can face them more easily.

if you're someone who worries that your style of helping might be disempowering your staff or clients, or if you're someone that believes that you can't say no (or really struggle to) or if you're someone that simply doesn't feel confident that you have what it takes to nurture others, then you've already understood what's holding you back from nurturing others. And that means that you're ready to start building in the mindset, the processes and the systems that will help you to really do just that.

This is the *how* to making care your competitive advantage. And embracing these elements will let you really embrace care into your business or practice so you can see all the amazing results that it will bring now and into the future.

Let's get started.

CHAPTER 3

MAKING CARE YOUR COMPETITIVE ADVANTAGE

Introduction

In the first chapter of this book, we examined *why* nurturing ourselves, our customers and our team matters (and there are so many reasons why it does!). In chapter 2 we talked about the things that might hold us back from really providing care to our teams and clients. Now we need to understand what the right kind of nurturing can look like in our business. In other words, how can we make care our competitive advantage?

When I think about what nurturing looks like in business, I picture Alena Bennett, who is a valued member of our community. She has a thriving practice and has worked with CFOs for a number of years. She is very clear on exactly who she works with, who she leads and who she cares for. She has the mindset of creating a CFO of the future.

Alena has created diagnostics and is incredibly focused on helping her clients achieve their potential. She is generous in the resources, tools, advice and one-on-one time she gives them. She also publishes her *CFO Insights* report every year. These are some ways that Alena has built a culture of care within her practice. But she doesn't do it on her own.

Importantly, Alena also has the staff, systems and tools in place to support her mission, because she can't do all of the work by herself. And rather than take all that work upon herself (and ultimately burn out), she focuses on making sure that her team can support her in her vision to create a culture of care for her clients.

Alena is a perfect example of how to put the Model of Care into practice.

Model of Care

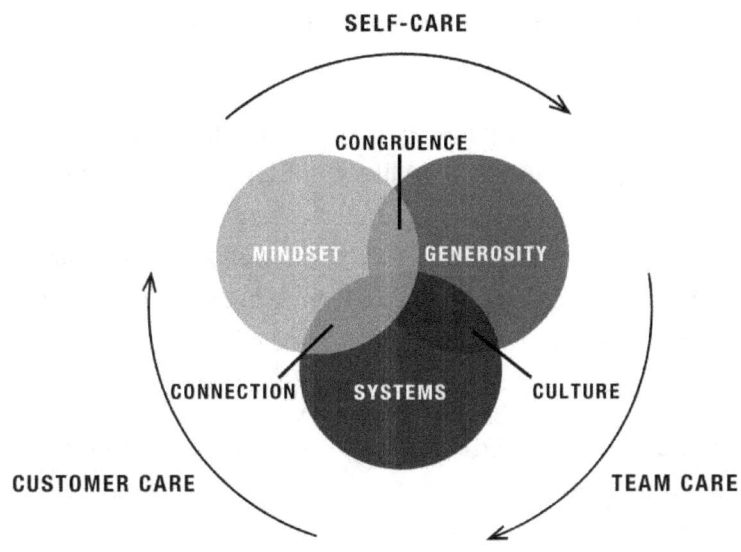

The Model of Care shows us what nurture should look like in a business or practice in order to create an overarching culture of care and establish it as a competitive advantage.

As you can see, the outer ring shows us the relationships it covers, those being self-care, team care and customer care. Next we see the three key components that help to create a sense of care and nurturing in each of those relationships, which include mindset, generosity and systems. And finally, we find the intersections of components and relationships which give you congruence, culture and connection.

Let's explore this Model of Care more thoroughly.

Self-care, team care, customer care

This outermost level of our Model of Care shows the relationships that we need to focus on in our practice or business. After Chapter 1, we already understand all the benefits of providing care to our team, our customers and even ourselves. So focusing on building our practice or business to support those relationships makes sense – both from a sustainability and ROI perspective.

If your business is leaving you feeling overworked, overburdened and burnt out (or nearly!), then you're likely not focusing enough on your own self-care. If you're struggling to attract and retain good talent in your business, then you're likely not putting enough care into your team. And if you're finding that you're having to attract new clients all the time, or are failing to keep your current clients happy, then you might need to focus more on your customer care.

These relationships all need nurture in order for your business to be truly successful.

Mindset, generosity, systems

In level 2, we start looking at how to actually create that care in your business. And to do that you need three main components – mindset, generosity and systems.

Mindset

You've likely heard a lot about mindset in your business. But in order to truly nurture your relationships in your business, mindset is the first (and arguably most important) step.

In order to care, we need to have a mindset of 'attention out' rather than 'attention in' – something that can be extremely difficult when it comes to your livelihood.

Of course, this is not to say that we shouldn't be commercially minded. But we can't be focussed solely on our business' success. Because having a mindset of care is part of what will drive that success.

Having a mindset of care then needs to become part of the culture of your business. This perspective needs to be kept at the top of your mind no matter what you're doing in your business. It needs to be part of what drives your every decision, as well as the mission, values and goals of your brand and be the guiding light of every step your team makes.

In other words, your mindset of care needs to be worked into the very fabric of your business or practice.

Generosity

The second component of the second level is to be generous. When it comes to being generous some relationships are easier than others. For example, it's likely easier to be generous to your clients, then it is to yourself. Or if not 'easier' then perhaps more natural.

But when it comes to generosity as part of the Model of Care, this is a vital part of each relationship you have in your business or practice – whether that's your relationship with yourself, with your team or with your customers.

Most of the coaches and consultants I work with are premium providers. They generally charge their clients more, but they also have excellent reputations for being generous. In effect, they offer great value to their clients and always make sure they're helping them get what they need. Sometimes that may be a little extra time or attention. Sometimes that might mean some additional advice or sharing of resources. Whatever the need, these premium providers look at insights and ways they can guide and educate their clients to help them take steps towards achieving their goals.

This same approach needs to be taken for your team. You need to be giving your time and expertise to your team, to allow them to grow and develop in a way that supports their wellbeing. And this approach needs to be taken for yourself as well. To be generous with yourself may be the hardest element of nurturing. But it will also see you developing a business that will support you into the future.

Systems

While your mindset and generosity are vital components of building care into your business systems are what support you to actually accomplish it.

A person – no matter how motivated – can't do all of this on their own. Having systems and tools in place ensures that your approach to care is built into the processes and procedures of your business. It ensures that every member of your team is cultivating that same behaviour in your business.

Systems will ensure that the rhythms, routines and cadences are all set up so that it is very clear to you and your team what needs to be done to be able to nurture yourself, your team and your clients. It's not always a natural default for people. But systems allow it to be learned and implemented easily. Of course, you need to have the right systems in place first (but we'll cover that in the remaining chapters).

Intersections in the Model of Care

When you're working with the model of care, the elements of level 2 aren't the results you're striving for themselves. In other words, while you need mindset and systems to achieve a culture of care, their real benefit lies in the results they create for you inside your business or practice. And those results lie at the intersections of the elements.

Congruence: If you've got mindset and generosity working, then you will achieve congruence in terms of feeling aligned and authentic to the customer. These two parts working together mean that the practice is not just being generous for the sake of selling more products or services – but with the purpose of serving and supporting its customers.

Culture: If you've got generosity and systems working, then you will create a culture within your business and practice that is built around nurturing. This is the basis for your culture of care for your customers and team members. This allows your business to position itself and have that competitive advantage because customers will be attracted to it.

Connection: If you've got the mindset and systems in place, then you will remain connected to your customers and help them to feel valued. It becomes a lot like a magnet in that your clients will become really attracted to you and come to you. And when you have real connection, retention becomes much easier. In fact, your clients will become very hard to lose. They're going to stay with you for a long time, if not forever.

Care: Take a look at the model closely and you will see that at the heart of the diagram sits 'care' – and that is where you want your practice to be. This is where mindset, generosity and systems all intersect, meaning all three components of the model are working effectively. This is the ultimate goal, and an excellent example of this is my client, Alena.

Why Does the Model of Care Work?

People want to feel valued

In 2007, a fantastic social experiment crafted by *The Washington Post* saw one of the world's greatest musicians busk in a metro station during the morning rush hour.[1] Dressed in casual clothes but armed with a violin reported to be worth around US$3.5 million, Joshua Bell played six classical pieces, including a piece said to be one of the most difficult violin pieces to master. More than 1,000 people passed by – but very few of them stopped, or even turned their heads. After 43 minutes, Joshua has made only $32.17.

There are many observations we can draw from this experiment, but one that seems startlingly obvious to me is that our environment can shape how much we are valued. On that cold morning in the station, the internationally acclaimed virtuoso was largely ignored. But just three days earlier, he had filled Boston's Symphony Hall, with seats selling for around $100 each. He has recorded more than 40 albums, earning GRAMMY®, Mercury® and Gramophone awards.

As business leaders, the Model of Care helps us to apply this lesson in our practices. We need to ensure that our people are in the most supportive environment possible, where their talents are recognised and celebrated. We want to see our staff and clients thrive, not go unnoticed.

And of course, they want that for themselves too. Customer experience futurist Blake Morgan compiled 50 statistics from an array of different studies that showed just how important a good customer experience is for business.[2] She highlighted research that found companies that lead

---

[1] Weingarten, G. (2007, April 8). Pearls Before Breakfast: Can one of the nation's great musicians cut through the fog of a D.C. rush hour? Let's find out. *The Washington Post.* https://www.washingtonpost.com/lifestyle/magazine/pearls-before-breakfast-can-one-of-the-nations-great-musicians-cut-through-the-fog-of-a-dc-rush-hour-lets-find-out/2014/09/23/8a6d46da-4331-11e4-b47c-f5889e061e5f_story.html?itid=lk_inline_manual_4.

[2] Morgan, B. (2019, September 24). 50 Stats That prove The Value Of Customer Experience. *Forbes.*
https://www.forbes.com/sites/blakemorgan/2019/09/24/50-stats-that-

in customer experience outperformed their competitors by almost 80%, while 84% of companies that work to improve their customer experience report a boost in revenue. Similarly, brands with superior customer experience bring in 5.7 times more revenue than brands that don't, and customer-centric companies are 60% more profitable than their competitors.

Make care your competitive advantage. When we nurture our customers, look after them and find ways to keep them, this can not only lead to sales growth but also save the time and money usually spent looking for new customers. Often, we have great customers right under our noses but we simply haven't taken the time to consider who they are, what they need and how we can help them further.

It's time to build loyalty and leadership

As Edward Albert once said, 'The simple act of caring is heroic.' This holds true for us in business – while some may not understand the value of caring for the customer, we must rise above the noise and keep nurturing anyway. It may not be easy to measure the returns on nurturing your clients, but I believe it's a long-term investment that can bring great rewards.

In doing so, you might also end up positioning yourself as a leader in your field. 'Leaders' are people who genuinely care and strive to bring out the best in others – often mentoring and inspiring them to achieve great goals. At the core of human potential is a need to feel like you're experiencing growth and taking steps towards your ambitions. If you can tap into that need for people to belong and grow every day, then

---

prove-the-value-of-customer-experience/?sh=3eeac4e44ef2#:~:text=Companies%20with%20a%20customer%20experience,outperform%20laggards%20by%20nearly%2080%25.

you can position yourself in a really unique way that encourages your clients to want to stay with you for a long time into the future.

On the flipside, if you don't nurture your clients, there will be no genuine connection and the relationship may feel transactional. Your customers may feel like you only see them as a commodity and not a person. This lack of emotional connection to you as a person and as a brand will impact on their sense of loyalty – and they may instead become focused on price and getting 'a good deal'. This of course may drive them to look elsewhere.

In a nutshell, if you don't care for your clients, someone else will.

Conclusion

Creating a culture of care within your business comes down to having an effective Model of Care in place – that is, making sure you have mindset, generosity and the appropriate systems operating smoothly. You and your team must know your ideal customer, be generous in your support of them and have your tools and systems in place to support the behaviours you're looking for.

In the following chapter, we will investigate *how* you can implement the Model of Care to enjoy a competitive advantage.

CHAPTER 4

EMBRACING SELF-CARE

While most of us will have heard the proverb, 'You can't pour from an empty cup', it's unlikely that we heed its advice in our daily lives. In fact, when it comes to our practices and businesses, we almost invariably put our clients and customers' needs above our own. We likely think we're doing the right thing, and see this as 'caring' for them. But the reality is that in order to truly take care of others, you first need to look after yourself.

If you can get the balance right – that is, caring for yourself as well as for others – you'll be on your way to creating a sustainable business that will last a lifetime and in creating loyal clients that want to stick with you for the long term. That's because self-care gives you the energy you need to be able to focus on others, but in a truly nurturing way.

Researchers believe that regularly taking care of ourselves, however that looks for you, helps you to react better to the things that go on in your life, and helps you to put your best foot forward in general.[1] And studies show that self-care helps leaders to manage the demands in their work life, reduce their stresses overall and protect their resources.[2]

---

[1] Lawler, M. (2023). *What Is Self-Care, and Why Is It So Important for Your Health?* Available at https://www.everydayhealth.com/self-care/.

[2] Klug K, Felfe J and Krick A. (2022). Does Self-Care Make You a Better Leader? A Multisource Study Linking Leader Self-Care to Health-Oriented Leadership,

On the other hand, if you don't get the balance right by practising thoughtful self-care, you could be setting yourself up for overwhelm, stress and even burnout.[3] And if you find yourself in that situation, you could find your performance reduced, your ability to focus impaired and your business struggling overall.[4]

Monique's Story

Monique Richardson is a great example of someone who learned to practise self-care and made her business far more sustainable because of it. Monique is a leading Australian expert in customer service. She has worked with thousands of customer service professionals, from senior management to frontline and support teams. When she came into my community she truly was at the top of her game. But she was also facing burn out.

Monique and her husband have four children. As an incredibly nurturing person, she wanted to give her all to both her family and her clients. But was concerned about being able to be her best self at home *or* at work. She was stretched and being pulled in a lot of directions. Her business – and life –needed to be sustainable.

Employee Self-Care, and Health. *Int J Environ Res Public Health*. Available at https://www.ncbi.nlm.nih.gov/pmc/articles/PMC9180678/.

[3] *Signs you might be experiencing a burnout and how to regain balance in your life.* (2021). Queensland Government: Darling Downs Health. Available at https://www.darlingdowns.health.qld.gov.au/about-us/our-stories/feature-articles/signs-you-might-be-experiencing-a-burnout-and-how-to-regain-balance-in-your-life#:~:text=Burnout%20is%20a%20state%20of,an%20increasing%20sense%20of%20hopelessness.

[4] Signs you might be experiencing a burnout and how to regain balance in your life. (2021). Queensland Government: Darling Downs Health.

So I asked her what one thing she would love to delegate, even if it seemed indulgent.

Monique thought about it for a while, but then finally said that a private chef four days a week, to cook nutritious food for her family, would give her back her time and energy while supporting the life and business that she wanted. For Monique, it was the ultimate self-care.

So we set about investigating it as an option. And as we ultimately discovered, a private chef was actually more affordable than she thought.

So Monique gave it a go, and it turned out to be a game changer. Not having to think about – or spend time preparing – nightly meals came with huge practical benefits for her, her clients and her family. She ended up being able to give more to her clients and to her family, and feel more fully present for both. Her business suddenly became far more sustainable.

Burnout is the result of a failure to exercise self-care

The World Health Organization listed exhaustion and burnout as an occupational syndrome in 2019 saying:

'Burn-out is a syndrome conceptualized as resulting from chronic workplace stress that has not been successfully managed. It is characterised by three dimensions:

1. feelings of energy depletion or exhaustion;
2. increased mental distance from one's job, or feelings of negativism or cynicism related to one's job; and
3. reduced professional efficacy.'[5]

---

[5] (28 May 2019). 'Burn-out an "occupational phenomenon": International Classification of Diseases'. World Health Organization: Departmental News.

Within my own community I've seen how debilitating burnout can actually be. We've got to do everything we can to prevent it as it can truly undermine our ability to care for others, and perform in our work. But to do that we have to embrace our own self-care. And we have to do it everyday.

Implementing self-care into your business

To implement self-care into your business, it takes more than just a recognition of its importance. You have to have:

1. A **mindset** of self-care
2. A **generosity** towards yourself
3. The **systems** to support your own self-care

Mindset

Nurturing your self-care, takes the ability to see yourself as a pivotal component of your business. We often ignore this, with family, kids, responsibilities and life taking over. But we have to remember that we ALWAYS have a choice. And this choice is where we create the ability to do things differently from how they have been done before.

Just as accepting self-care as an important part of her business strategy (and life strategy!) helped Monique to grow her own business, and find flow and sustainability, a mindset of self-care of self-care will get you there as well.

Here's how to start developing a mindset of self-care.

Available at https://www.who.int/news/item/28-05-2019-burn-out-an-occupational-phenomenon-international-classification-of-diseases.

Do what you love – let go of what you don't

Developing a mindset of self-care in your business first starts with understanding what you love – and what you don't. So, my first question is, what brings you joy every day? What do you love to do that sparks your excitement, enthusiasm, happiness and brings you energy?

For me, it's dogs. I love my dog Winston, and I love everybody else's dogs. I love the cuddles and puppy love. In fact, I even dog-sit sometimes. And every day I take Winston down to the dog park.

We don't go to the dog park because Winston has such a good time. He likes it fine – but he just likes to sniff around. I, on the other hand, get a lot out playing with the dogs.

I love all the different breeds. I love their personalities. I love all the cuddles and throwing balls to chase. It's just so much fun. This is an hour that I do something just for myself. I love that once a day I can just settle into doing something that I love. And I can't get enough of it. It puts me in a really good mood.

When I've had that hour with the dogs then I carry that 'feel good' feeling with me throughout the rest of the working week. I feel really switched on and good when I'm talking to my clients. And when I'm like that then my clients get the best out of me.

My second question is, how do you carve out time for yourself? Are you blocking time in your calendar? Are you looking at the time that needs to go in every quarter or every week?

I personally block a week off of client-facing work once every quarter. I've found that this is the time that I need to recoup. I need time to recharge and disconnect. I might go to the beach for a couple of days. I might go and get a massage. I just might want to clean up my office to make it more conducive to work in. I might get some fresh flowers, do a big spring clean, and just make it feel beautiful and productive again.

For me, I know that my physical space has an impact on my ability to work. So part of my self-care is to carve out the time to ensure I keep it looking nice and feeling good.

The final question is, what do you say no to? How do you prioritise? What are your boundaries? And how easy do you find that to do? Another way to think about that is, how do you make sure you're saying yes to the right things?

This is the time for you to let go of the things that aren't working for you. This might be setting work boundaries in the time and space that you'll be 'on'. This might be saying no to certain kinds of projects or certain kinds of clients. It can also be outsourcing some elements of your business – bookkeeping for example – or parts of your life – such as Monique did when she hired a private chef.

If you can work out the answers to these things – the things that you love and the things that you don't – you're going to have a mindset of self-care so that you really can nurture and bring out the best in others.

Self-worth and self esteem

Sometimes when it comes to self-care, the thing that gets the most in the way is our own self-worth. This is our belief that we are important enough to care about.

I love the quote from L.R. Knost, international best-selling and award-winning author and child development researcher, where she says, 'Taking care of myself doesn't mean "me first." It means "me, too".'

I love this because you are important. You are just as important as every other team member in your organisation. You are just as important as every one of your clients.

It's not about you coming first – but it's also not about you coming last. It's about you treating your needs as equal to those of your team and your customers. It's giving yourself the same care that you would give to anyone else.

Sometimes when I'm working with women they have the fear that by caring for others they may go too far and lose themselves in the process. They worry that they're going to focus too much on everyone else, and that means they'll be last in the office, last to go home, last to sleep. Their concern is that they're going to be the one carrying the load because they've been too worried about everybody else.

When Monique first thought about getting a chef to help her in the home and free up her time and mental space, one thing that held her back was the idea that it was simply too indulgent. She said to me, 'It's easy to feel like this could be an indulgent thing. Only celebrities do this stuff.' But once she looked into it, she knew that it could be a gamechanger for her business – and it was.

It's important to recognise that nurturing is a different animal. It's about care that creates opportunity for growth and development and that applies to you as well. You can't let yourself be held back because you're worried that it might be seen as indulgent or too much. You can't fail to nurture yourself because you're worried that it might be putting yourself first.

You are worth it.

Self-esteem is about seeing yourself as enough and good enough, and these feelings can develop and change at different stages in your life for different reasons. If you're struggling to feel good about yourself it might be because you're going through a change. It could be a new job. It could be in your midlife where you start to realise you have less skills or fewer abilities than you probably thought you did. Or perhaps later in life you might feel like you're just not relevant anymore (which is patently untrue!).

When you have self-esteem, you tend to be more courageous. You tend to value your time. But when you have low self-esteem, you may feel like you want to hide. You don't want to see anyone. You may even suffer from imposter syndrome, fearing that you might somehow be found out.

This isn't uncommon. Low self-esteem can happen to anyone – even someone like Audrey Hepburn. Audrey Hepburn was known for her beauty, elegance and talent, and she achieved a lot of great success in Hollywood. In fact, she became one of the most celebrated actresses of her time.

But despite her outward appearance of confidence and grace, she battled with self-esteem and the imposter syndrome for a long time. A lot of it stemmed from her time during childhood in World War II, where she lived in the Netherlands. She suffered from malnutrition and the trauma of witnessing the atrocities of war, which had a lasting impact on her self-image.

She was very conscious about how tall she was, and felt that she didn't fit the traditional standards of beauty during that time. She didn't feel like she was really living up to the expectations set by her success. She once said, 'I was asked to act when I couldn't act. I was asked to sing "Funny Face" when I couldn't sing, and dance with Fred Astaire when I couldn't dance – and do all kinds of things I wasn't prepared for. Then I tried like mad to cope with it.'

Despite her self doubt, audiences were wowed. And because of that she was able to focus on other things that she loved. She did incredible humanitarian work and became a UNICEF Goodwill Ambassador. She's a good reminder that it doesn't matter how successful you are, struggles with self-esteem can often be something that will come along and affect you.

So how can you bolster your self-esteem and feelings of self-worth?

1. Ask yourself what your values are and what's important to you? Focus on those in your life.
2. Determine your ratio of positive to negative self-talk? Then work on improving that ratio. And work on improving your self-talk. Louise Hay, who is the author of multiple books said, 'You have been criticizing yourself for years and it hasn't worked. Try approving of yourself and see what happens.'(Read the section on self-talk to learn more.)
3. Think about who you are hanging out with? Who are the people you're surrounding yourself with? Do they help you feel stronger, validated and worthy? If not, you might need to consider changing the company that you keep.

Be detached and light

Part of your self-care mindset is to be deliberately detached. This doesn't mean that you don't care – in fact, you care very much. But having a certain level of detachment is how you can both care for your clients and customers, and for yourself at the same time.

One of the things I grew up loving to watch was car racing. I really enjoyed anything like the V8, Formula 1 and even rally driving. I always found rally driving kind of interesting because the driver can't operate on their own. They have to work together with the navigator in order to see the bends, work out where they've got to go and ultimately be successful.

If you've got clients who are struggling, a sense of detachment will help you care, but not rescue. And that's a vital distinction.

A rescuer will say things like, 'Look, I'm not going to charge you. We're going to do all this extra work. We're going to fix it. I'll make sure it's all OK.' But when you rescue, you're taking it all on yourself – the responsibility and the care and the ultimate outcome. And that's simply too much. There's only one of you and you can only do so much. And when you try to do too much you can exhaust yourself and burn yourself out, in which case you're not going to be good to anybody.

On the other hand, the carer will say, 'I'm just going to take some pressure off you. I'm here to help. I'm here to support you. You'll have to pay for the work but I'm going to stop the payments for now and take that pressure off. I'm here to help you when you need it'. As a carer you won't be falling over and losing yourself in someone else's problem. You help, but you also keep the boundary between what you can do to help and what you can't very clear.

This is the line you have to walk. But to do that you have to be able to practise deliberate detachment.

When you practise deliberate detachment you care about your customer and their business but not more than they do. If you find that you care about it more than they do, then you aren't deliberately detached, and you may need to walk away.

I had a coaching client once who had particular messaging that she was sending out in her branding. It was the total opposite of what I advised her to do and I believed it was the reason her business wasn't growing.

During her coaching sessions, we talked in great detail about her messaging and each time I gave her feedback that I didn't recommend it. In fact, I told her that she was repelling people and hurting her business in the process. But she didn't want to hear it.

In our final session, she said, 'I know it's not what you want to hear, but I'm going to keep doing this because I like it.' And I said, 'OK. That's absolutely your choice. But in this case, since you're not implementing what I'm suggesting, I don't think I'm going to be able to help you. So I'm not going to be able to continue working with you.'

I could have kept on helping of course. I could have said, 'OK, well, I'm going to try and help you and help you grow your business even though

I can see very clearly that you don't want to implement what I'm saying, so it's really a waste of time, money, energy, effort and me coaching you.'

But I would have been caring more about her business than she was herself. I would have lost my ability to be deliberately detached, and that would turn me into a rescuer. She had to come to the realisation herself that her messaging wasn't working.

As Deepak Chopra says, 'The Law of Detachment says that in order to acquire anything in the physical universe, you have to relinquish your attachment to it. This doesn't mean that you give up the intention to create your desire. You don't give up the intention, and you don't give up the desire. You give up your attachment to the result.'

I think he's right. To achieve anything, you've got to hold it lightly. It's not good for anyone to be obsessed with a single result or project and to hold it so tightly that you'll try to control it at all costs. You can't control everything because every outcome is not up to you. There will be other people that have input and some control. So, it's best to put it in the universe and work for it – but ensure you remain deliberately detached.

This is also a form of self-care. Your detachment allows you to move forward in your life and your business without becoming bogged down in one thing – one project, one customer or one person.

To practise deliberate detachment as yourself:

1. What are you wanting to master? What are you wanting most for your customers and your team?
2. Are you caring too much? Are you falling into rescuing?
3. How close are you sitting to deliberate detachment? What do you need to do to let go and relinquish control a little bit?

You're not for everyone (so care for those who matter most)

Steve Jobs famously said, 'If you want to make everyone happy, don't be a leader, sell ice cream.' As part of your mindset of self care, you'll want to understand one thing very well – you're not for everyone... and that's OK. (Because if you wanted to be for everyone, you would go sell ice cream!)

When we're in the midst of building our leadership, our position will be changing. Where we might have felt like part of the team, or close to colleagues or friends before, it will feel differently now.

Of course, it's natural to want to stay connected, to feel like you belong or like you're hanging out with your friends. But sometimes you may find that you have the wrong people around you. So, to grow and change you must consider letting go of those people. This might mean letting go of suppliers, members of your team or even your customers. But this letting go is a sign of evolution – a sign that you're growing and changing.

Having the wrong people around you is not ideal. It can pull you down into quicksand pretty quickly and create a toxic environment for your colleagues, team members and customers. On the other hand, if you really hone in on those who are a good fit for you, then you create the time and space that allows you to innovate, progress, create and grow.

In the early 2000s HP acquired a business called EDS. But though they had acquired it to help grow the enterprise side of their business, integrating it into HP was much harder than they expected. As it turned out the culture of the two companies were very different and the clients they helped were very different. Over time the integration just became far too complex and difficult, so they ended up selling it. They realised they just needed to focus on those they were a good fit for.

Understanding that you're not for everyone is an important part of your self-care as a leader. But that's not always easy to accept. Matthew Lieberman, professor in the Departments of Psychology, Psychiatry and Biobehavioral Sciences at the University of California, Los Angeles, completed research about our need to belong which he shared in his TedX talk. He said, leaders who are results-focused aren't usually seen as great leaders. But leaders that are results-focused *and* also have strong social skills have a much greater chance of being seen as a great leader.[6] But for us as leaders, it's something that we often grapple with because we're not necessarily trying to fit in.

In the book, *The Courage to be Disliked*, the authors Ichiro Kishimi and Fumitake Koga give us a philosophy on how to have the courage to live a happy, authentic life. Their advice centers on retraining your mind to accept yourself as you are. And once you can do this, you can also accept others as they are. This is part of the key to understanding that you're not for everyone.

So, the questions for you to consider are:

1. If you're not for everyone who do you need to let go of? Is it certain customers? Maybe it's team members?
2. To grow and change you may need to have some uncomfortable conversations? Are you prepared for that?
3. Who are the right people to bring around you? If you're not for everyone (and you're not!) who are you for?

Longevity and sustainability

We often think about sustainability in terms of the environment and the planet. We even think about it for organisations. But we rarely apply the

---

[6] Lieberman, M. (2013). *The Social Brain and Its Superpowers*. 8 October 2013. TedX Talks. Available at https://www.youtube.com/watch?v=NNhk3owF7RQ.

same mindset to ourselves. We need to ask ourselves if what we're doing in work and in life is sustainable?

Understanding the answer to this question will help you to make decisions about your own long term self-care and ensure you have a sustainable business or practice. This will, therefore, give you the ability to cultivate and nurture your own teams and talent.

When you're operating in a sustainable version of yourself, it's kind of like tending to a flourishing garden. You're sowing seeds, pulling out weeds and cultivating that real vibrant garden that's happening. And it's the same for yourself. You need to make sure you're getting enough sleep, eating well and surrounding yourself with the right people. You'll want to ask yourself, do I have clarity in my work? Am I confident in what I'm doing? Do I know how to do this? How stressed am I? Am I dealing with work overload and overwhelm?

Jim Rohn, American entrepreneur, author and motivational speaker, said, 'You've got to take care of your body because it's the only place you have to live.'

This reminds me of Ally, who is in my community. She has four children under eight and is also running her own successful business. She's a very high energy person and is able to juggle a lot of things and so she's able to sustain stress and manage her time quite well. But pushing herself in this way just isn't sustainable. As I've said to her, 'You're going to have your business for a lifetime. So we have to try and work out how to make sure you're getting sleep and taking care of yourself too.'

For Ally this meant getting the right support to back her up in life and in business. This has made the difference between having a business that burns hot but then burns out (or sees Ally burning out) and having a business that is sustainable for the long term.

To find out if you have a sustainable business, ask yourself:

1. How are you feeling energy-wise right now? Is this a once off or does it happen all the time?
2. What will be the impact if this continues for the next week, month, year?
3. How are you going to get your business or practice back under control so that you can be doing your life's work?

Attitude of gratitude

When it comes to your mindset of self-care, one of the most important elements is having an attitude of gratitude. Within all the craziness and busyness of everyday, it can constantly feel like we just can't get everything done. And that feels as if it's widening the gap between where we are now and where we want to be. And it can just feel like there's never enough to go around.

But when you have an attitude of gratitude, it grounds into you what you do have. It reminds you of how far you've come, and it helps to reduce the overwhelm so you can become more present. It means that you show up with a different type of energy and you vibrate in a very different way. This then allows you to be more mindful about what you care about.

I remember seeing Dr Jason Fox, philosopher, speaker and leadership expert, speak at an event. During his speech he talked about how after going through an extreme growth in his practice, becoming an extremely in demand speaker and even writing a couple of books, he hit a point where he wondered, 'When is it supposed to be enough?'

He said, 'I feel like we're just growing. But I'm not really that happy. How am I supposed to nurture others when I feel like this?' He went on to say that the first thing he did was to just stop and talk to his wife each day about three things they were grateful for. It's a really simple thing, but it helped them to really determine that they were growing just for the sake of growth itself. And they were actually happy with what they already had. It was enough.

Martin Seligman, founder of the Positive Psychology Center at the University of Pennsylvania, found that spending five to 10 minutes each day for a week writing down three things that went well that day increased happiness for six months.[7] An incredible result. And this is just what Dr Fox found as well. Taking these steps changed his mindset – and because of that, is a vital form of self-care.

Eckhart Tolle, who has written quite a number of books and is an expert in presence, talks about how acknowledging the good you have in your life is the foundation for all abundance. I know this to be true, because when you can't or don't do that you can find yourself falling into a scarcity mindset.

When this happens then you start becoming focused on what's missing and what's wrong. You'll slip below the line and into a negative mindset. It might be hard to practise an attitude of gratitude – often it feels counterintuitive, particularly if you're being tough on yourself. But even if you aren't suffering from depression or another mental health issue, 80% of your self-talk is already negative.[8] 80%! So we have to constantly be on the lookout for ways to counteract that self-talk. And practising gratitude by writing down the three things you're most grateful for, is one way to do just that.

---

[7] Three Good Things. Greater Good Science Center: Magazine. Available at https://www.google.com/url?q=http://ggia.berkeley.edu/practice/three-good-things%23data-tab-evidence&sa=D&source=docs&ust=1691127838828709&usg=AOvVaw3CPxdN-vS8AFxOJ9qL7Vse.

[8] Simone, F. (4 December 2017). 'Negative Self-Talk: Don't Let It Overwhelm You'. *Psychology Today.* Available at https://www.psychologytoday.com/us/blog/family-affair/201712/negative-self-talk-dont-let-it-overwhelm-you.

Mindset of abundance

As we said above, having an attitude of gratitude is the foundation for abundance, and when you're nurturing, you've got to have a mindset of abundance.

Abundance in your work or practice is like being in an ocean. There's so much available to us. There's so much there. But unfortunately we tend to stand on the shoreline, playing in the small waves that come to us. We look at all the other people standing on the shore as well and worry that there's not enough for everyone. We stop looking out into the deep.

In the same way, we tend to focus on the people right in front of us, the potential pool of customers that it seems like everyone is competing for. And because of that we worry that there's not enough. There's not enough customers or clients. There's not enough money. There's not enough of anything. And this fear and scarcity mindset can hold us back from stepping into care, because we have a fear that we don't have enough time, we don't have enough clients, we don't have enough money or there's not enough talent in the market.

But with a mindset of abundance we can come to realise just how much is out there, and your growth will come. For example, if you've got a staff member and they're not performing, you might have a fear that if you let them go, you'll never find anyone else. This is a scarcity mindset. But if you have an attitude of abundance then you can recognise when you've tried everything, and you can recognise when it might be time to let them go. And it's only when you do let them go that you can open yourself up for the opportunities that the right team member will bring. It's only by creating the space for them that you can truly grow.

Bryant McGill, thought leader, international bestselling author, activist, social entrepreneur and one of the world's top social media influencers, says, 'Abundance is a process of letting go; that which is empty can receive.' So you've got to create space in order to receive.

Of course sometimes we may find that we don't have either abundance or space. In that case you've got to think big. Yale did a study on middle-aged adults, and found that those people who have more positive beliefs around ageing live longer. So those who believed that they would live longer, actually did. They lived seven and a half years longer.[9]

So when you're thinking about nurturing and growing and building abundance, instead of feeling like, 'I can't afford to do that.' Or, 'I don't have time', you can think, 'Well, there is the time and I do have the right clients.' Don't focus too small.

Ask yourself:

1. What are you feeling most scared about, or most scarce about? Is it time, money, sales, staff, clients?
2. What's holding you back from being able to care for your clients? Is it that you fear that you're not going to have enough energy or time for yourself or your family?

Once you can shift your mindset and think about how you can actually create time yourself and make that the priority then you'll find yourself open to abundance and open to growth. And that is the ultimate mindset of self care.

Generosity

Once you have your self-care mindset in place, you can then accept that it's something that is both important to your business and important to your life. And because of that, you have to be willing to be generous with yourself – and allow yourself the opportunities to pursue that self-care.

---

[9] Levy, B, Slad, M, Kunkel, S and Kasl, S. (2002). 'Longevity increased by positive self-perceptions of aging'. *Journal of Personality and Social Psychology*. Available at https://pubmed.ncbi.nlm.nih.gov/12150226/.

Here's some ways to be generous to yourself.

Time

First, be generous with yourself on time. One of the most common things we do in business is underestimate how long things take to do. When we don't give ourselves enough time to do our work, we're not valuing ourselves. You've got to be realistic about how long things take and give yourself the time and space to actually do it.

My dad is an accountant and he does my bookkeeping with me. It drives me insane because he says, 'Oh, when we catch up, we'll just do this and we'll have a look at this. It'll only take five minutes.' Everything in my dad's world takes five minutes. But it doesn't take five minutes. It takes an hour and a half, or it takes two hours. Sometimes we'll be sitting there still for a bit longer.

My dad isn't alone in underestimating the time things can take. We often kid ourselves on how long things take, and because of that we undervalue ourselves by not giving ourselves enough time to get things done. Researchers call this the 'planning fallacy' – which states that people continually underestimate the time it will take them to complete a task (though not other people).[10]

As Matthew Kelly says in his book, *The Long View*, 'Most people overestimate what they can do in a day, and underestimate what they can do in a month. We overestimate what we can do in a year, and underestimate what we can accomplish in a decade.'

---

[10] Buehler, R, Griffin, D. & Ross, M. (September 1994). 'Exploring the "Planning Fallacy": Why People Underestimate Their Task Completion Times'. *Journal of Personality and Social Psychology*. Available at https://www.researchgate.net/publication/232558487_Exploring_the_Planning _Fallacy_Why_People_Underestimate_Their_Task_Completion_Times.

When you're generous with yourself and allow yourself enough time to get tasks done (and done properly) then it's like a gentle breeze that gracefully fills the sails of a boat to allow it to effortlessly cross the ocean. There's no friction. It's just smooth. It's effortless, and you're able to get things done.

The key here is being really conscious and aware of how long things take for you in general. You might have to spend some time paying attention to how long things actually take. Then as you cultivate a consciousness of time and space and how you work, you'll really develop the skill of estimating time and space and being able to be generous with yourself.

So ask yourself:

1. What are the three most important things that you need to do today?
2. How much time will each of those take?
3. And have you blocked time to do them? Because if there's no time blocked to do them, they're not necessarily going to happen.

Getting the right support around you

Regardless of whether you have the title of CEO or manager or not everybody has the ability to be a leader. But to do this we need to bring the right people around us. However, if you don't get the right support, you'll struggle because you'll feel quite alone and self-reliant. And when you're in that position, you can lose confidence very quickly.

On the other hand, if you have got the right support around you, it really does mean that anything is possible. And this is the highest form of self-care.

Janine Garner wrote the book, *It's Who You Know*. In it she talks about the 12 key people you need to have around you in your career and business. Among these 12 key people are people like butt kickers and teachers and mentors and pit crew – each has a job or a role to play in your success. So it's important to think about who really has the impact on your success and then work out how to prioritise those people in your life and ensure that you cultivate and nurture those relationships so you do have that support around you.

When you have the right support it's like having a floaty in the pool. Because you have it you're not going to sink or drown. And this holds true in your business as well. As Jim Rohn says, 'You are the average of the five people you spend the most time with.' And if they are the right people, that means you'll get the right support.

Robin Dunbar, a social anthropologist and researcher, took a look at ancient tribes, and noted that those that survived for many many generations have had leaders who kept a group of tribal elders around them. These elders acted as advisors and mentors and they helped that leader to lead the tribe through difficulties and survive. In the same way, your support team can help your business achieve the longevity and legacy that you deserve.

Self-talk

How you speak to yourself has a huge impact on how you care for yourself. When we are our own cheerleader and best friend, we tend to feel stronger and more resilient, and we'll be able to manifest greater possibilities than you could perhaps imagine.

On the other hand, if we're beating ourselves up all the time, we can become depressed, sad and frustrated. And when you're in that position you're certainly not going to be in a strong position to nurture others.

Self-talk is a big part of self care. And – as we mentioned earlier – 80% of our self-talk is negative. And this can really affect you. In order to nurture others, you have to start by nurturing yourself. You have to become your own best friend. And that starts with positive self talk.

When I got divorced and separated from my husband, I really struggled a lot with my confidence. So I started to work with a counsellor. And the first thing that she picked up was about my self-talk. She said, 'Do you realise that you put yourself down a lot? You've got to catch your own self-talk.' She was right of course. As Brene Brown said, 'Talk to yourself like you would to someone you love.' And the first step to doing that is catching your self-talk.

As soon as you hear yourself putting yourself down or saying anything negative, you need to stop and take note. These could be things like, 'I'm such an idiot.' Or, 'I'm so stupid.' Or, 'I just mess everything up.' You have to really pull yourself up, because sometimes it becomes so ingrained that we don't even really 'hear' it anymore.

Once you start to catch your negative self-talk, the next step is to rephrase it. So instead of saying, 'I mess everything up,' say, 'It's OK. I made a mistake. Everyone makes mistakes.' Or you could say, 'It's OK. Tomorrow's a new day.' Or you could say, 'I'm learning.' Those sorts of rephrases and affirmations can really help as well.

Another way to start to have better self-talk (and so better self-care) is to think about what you want to manifest, what you want to create, and write five affirmations on your bathroom mirror that you can repeat every night. This will help you to embed them in your subconscious and make a real change to how you speak to yourself.

Be generous to yourself

In talking and working with clients, I know that being generous to yourself is a mindset many find hard to adopt. It can feel self-indulgent and excessive. But as Audre Lord, feminist and civil rights activist said, 'caring for myself is not self-indulgence, it is self-preservation.'

And it's therefore essential to elevating your practice.

There are four key ways to be generous to yourself within your practice.

1. *Be generous with delegation*

I regularly ask clients what they could delegate to create more time to show up at their best. When we have our own practices or are in C-Suite roles, we often think that we can do it all ourselves. We might even think of delegating as an indulgence.

But delegating to create time and space for your own practice and to be a better version of yourself is not indulgent. It's a smart way to build sustainability in your work. That's because delegation allows you to create time and gives you space to focus your energies on the things that are most important in your life and in your practice.

2. *Block time to be generous with headspace*

Making the most of your time by 'blocking time' is an incredibly effective and efficient way to work. How many times have you heard people say they need more time, or there aren't enough hours in the day? We can't add more hours to the clock, but we can find ways to work smarter not harder, and give ourselves the generosity of headspace.

One example of blocking time is my Content Creation Bootcamp. In three days of intensive content creation, each participant completes 52 pieces of content – or 12 months of thought leadership. This focussed time and space enables you to think, plan and create in a supportive environment, while holding yourself accountable.

Another example could be quarterly planning sessions. Making the time each quarter to focus on your practice and what goals you'd like to achieve in the next quarter could give you the space you need.

3. *Be generous to your to-do list*

What does a generous 'to-do' list look like? It's a realistic list of what's actually achievable in your day or week that includes a little time to decompress between items or events. I find that too many people have to-do lists that overestimate what's practically possible in a given time frame. The to-list itself can be the cause of stress, which can incrementally add up, leading to burnout.

An honest, generous to-do list that builds in time between tasks to decompress or transition will help you to stay accountable. And you'll be able to achieve what's important and essential, and significantly, help you to avoid burnout.

4. Be generous by getting professional support

Finally, I can't recommend enough the importance of getting a coach, professional mentor or guide. Having someone to help you navigate your practice, allocate your time and understand when you may be headed for burnout, is absolutely key to your professional and personal success.

Celebrate wins

When it comes to self-care, it's important to celebrate your wins. When you celebrate wins, even small ones, you create a really positive mindset that shows that you value progress and will be mindful to support your team and customers in their own growth. If we wait to just celebrate the big wins, then it's going to feel like a long time between drinks. Your people won't feel like they're winning – and *you* won't feel like you're winning either. So celebrate wins even if they're small and celebrate regularly along the way.

When you celebrate the little winds it's a little bit like a sugar hit. It gets you that fix and will help release chemicals such as dopamine that make you (and your team and customers) feel good. This then keeps everyone motivated and we can even become addicted to that feeling of making progress.

Carol Dweck, preeminent researcher in growth mindset, says that celebrating these wins allows us to look back on how much effort we made and how far we've come and is so crucial to high performance. In essence it allows us to appreciate the journey, an important factor when building our own growth mindset.[11]

Fortunately, I grew up with my dad who celebrates the opening of an envelope. We would always be celebrating something, and they would often be small things. But they don't have to be big celebrations to make you feel good and honour your small accomplishments along your journey. Growing up my dad might suggest that we get some chocolate on the way home, or ice cream. Or we might go to the movies as a family. Small celebrations for small wins that made a huge impact in our lives. And my dad always had this positive way of seeing the value in those things.

Oprah Winfrey said, 'The more you praise and celebrate in your life, the more there is in life to celebrate.' And it's very true. You'll see that there are more positive things happening for you than negative things, and it will counteract the feelings of lack or overwhelm or the feeling that you're not getting anywhere.

So notice when things go well, don't just brush over them. Then celebrate. Be creative. Order dinner, flowers, treats, whatever. Life is worth living. You don't want it to be Groundhog Day all the time.

Systems

The final step in self-care is to have the systems in place to support your new self-care mindset and generous approach. And this starts with knowing your tribe.

---

[11] Dweck, C. (2017). Mindset: Changing The Way You Think To Fulfil Your Potential Paperback. Robinson.

Know your tribe and love them hard

The first most important part of your systems of self-care is to find your tribe and love them hard. So often we can spread ourselves way too thin when we're trying to grow a business. But if you take the time to slow down, focus a little more on what you're doing and find those people who are a good fit for you, you'll suddenly find yourself surrounded by 'your tribe' – those people who get you and support you and help you in your life and business.

Once you get them though, that's not the end game. You then need to pay attention to them and 'love them'. If you do you might be surprised how much of a response you'll get and the results that you'll see.

Years ago, I was speaking on stage with a very popular keynote speaker, Lisa McInnes-Smith, a lovely Australian lady. Lisa has spoken on some of the biggest stages around the world, including with presidents. She's a very well-seasoned speaker. In fact, she's one of the most experienced speakers in the country and also internationally. She's a certified speaking professional, one of only a few speakers in the world that have that certification, and she's also an inductee into the International Speaker Hall of Fame.

When we came off stage I asked her about her experiences. I said, 'Wow, you must do a lot to look after these bureaus, to have these sorts of speaking opportunities that come along.'

Her response surprised me when she said, 'No, not really. I really only work closely with two or three, but I love them and I love them hard.' I had thought that she must have a huge team who was looking after hundreds of bureaus, but it wasn't the case at all.

In the same way in our businesses and practices, we can sometimes think that more is better. But it's not necessarily true. Especially when it comes to the people around us. Danielle LaPorte, who's a transformation and personal development expert, says, 'Find your tribe. Love them hard.' And that means find the few and give them as much as you can.

So, how do you love your tribe hard?

1. First, identify who your people are. Who are your tribe, those people who are support you and give you insight and encouragement in your business and life.
2. Second, treat them like family. Make sure they understand they're a priority, and given the same amount of attention as they would get if they were blood relatives.
3. Third, stay in touch. Figure out the best way to stay in touch with them and execute it. Is it via text? Is it via phone? Is it via email? And what's the frequency?
4. Fourth, find out what's important to them. What floats their boat? What are the things they're into? What do they like doing? What are the things they do outside of work? Be curious enough to genuinely be interested in them as a person.
5. Fifth, share opportunities with them as things come along. Don't just hoard these for yourself. Find out how you could optimise these opportunities together and then make it happen.
6. Sixth, listen. Your tribe will sometimes have better ideas than you do. Embrace these. Learn from their experiences and take the opportunity to learn.
7. Seventh, be grateful. When your tribe finds opportunities for you or shares ideas and learnings with you, be grateful. Demonstrate this by sending them gifts or cards (or something else entirely!). Do what you can to really show you gratitude and show that you're very committed to their success and your success.

Find your 15 (your board of directors)

When you have a practice or a business, having the right people around you is vital (which is why we start with knowing your tribe!). When you have the right people around you, you will have more confidence, more conviction and more connection. Not just with your team, but also with your customers.

These 'strategic networks' give you greater influence, of course. But they also help you with your own self-care. That's because each person within your strategic network provides you with support and care that can get you through the rough times.

Researchers who performed a 10-year study found that people with a strong circle of friends were 22% less likely to die.[12] Another study at Harvard showed that strong social ties promoted brain health.[13] In other words, friendships can truly help you to live longer and think better.

This also applies to our strategic network. Your strategic network is your practice's lifeline. It makes your business more sustainable, helps it have longevity and actually helps you simply 'think' better when making decisions.

---

[12] Giles, L, Glonek, G, Luszcz, M & Andrews, G. 'Effect of social networks on 10 year survival in very old Australians: the Australian longitudinal study of aging'. [Research report]. *Journal of Epidemiology and Community Health.* Available at https://jech.bmj.com/content/59/7/574.abstract?maxtoshow=&HITS=10&hits=10&RESULTFORMAT=&fulltext=friends&andorexactfulltext=and&searchid=1&FIRSTINDEX=0&sortspec=date&resourcetype=HWCIT.

[13] Bilodeau, K. (8 September 2021). '3 ways to build brain-boosting social connections'. Harvard Health Publishing: Harvard Medical School. Available at https://www.health.harvard.edu/blog/3-ways-to-build-brain-boosting-social-connections-202109082585.

In a lot of ways, your strategic network is like your board of directors. They are the people that have the most impact and influence on your business or practice. They create the infrastructure around you that gives you both sustainability and support, either as a leader or even a team member.

Robin Dunbar's 15

Robin Dunbar is a social anthropologist who posited a layered approach to relationships.[14] In fact, his theory postulated that we have 15 (good friends), 150 (meaningful contacts), 500 (acquaintances) and 1500 (recognisable people). As part of this work he closely analysed tribes and leaders of tribes that were sustainable and survived the test of time.

In each case the tribal leader had about 15 tribal elders in their strategic network. These 15 elders performed the role of close friends and provided support as the leaders' performed their duties and in their personal lives. These 15 individuals provided the infrastructure the leader needed to support the wider community as well. In essence, they acted as the leader's strategic network.

Like these tribal leaders, each of us needs to find our own 15 people to form our strategic network. Without a strategic network around us it's easy to become lost, frustrated and disconnected. Just like life is harder without friends, our work and thought leadership will be stymied without a robust strategic network.

On the other hand, when we do have 15 people in our support network we'll find that we have cheerleaders, supporters, mentors, springboards, comforters and more. All the things we need to see us through all the ups and downs of work and life.

---

[14] 'Dunbar's number: Why we can only maintain 150 relationships'. *BBC Future*. Available at https://www.bbc.com/future/article/20191001-dunbars-number-why-we-can-only-maintain-150-relationships.

Who should be part of your 15?

To determine who should be part of your 15, we look back to Janine Garner's book, It's Who You Know. As we mentioned above, Janine identifies 12 key people you should have in your network. She describes them as promoters, pit crew, teachers and butt kickers – with three different levels under each of those categories.

Janine's analysis is a great place to start. From my experience, you also need to consider the people that might provide support for you and your unique situation. And the people that will allow you the opportunity to build self-care into your practice routine. So, for example, my 15 has more women than men, simply because it's been my experience that women provide the support that I need. You may have a different experience, or need different kinds of support. In that case, you'll need to look for the people who can provide that to you.

In addition, there is a difference between what men seem to need and what women seem to need when it comes to the strategic network. I've found that women tend to have three or four people around them to fulfil those roles. While men seem to put more focus into expanding their strategic network to embrace a full 15 people.

When you are ready to find your own 15, it comes down to identifying the people that you need around you, and bringing them into your life. So creating a strategic network involves using strategic wisdom.

Pearl Zhu, author of *Digitizing Boardroom*, says, 'Strategic wisdom is an integral, multidimensional intelligence.' You can think of it as using experience, knowledge and good judgement to create your plan of action. In this case, that's pulling together your own strategic network.

When Sarah started working with me she didn't know many people and she didn't have a lot of support around her. She was really good at what she did. But starting her own practice was a big risk for her, especially since she didn't have a support structure in place.

Chapter 4: **EMBRACING SELF-CARE** | 73

Working together we identified who she needed as a support in her new practice. She looked at her layers of relationships and found those that she needed in her top 15. So she really had to identify first her customer, and once she nailed that down, she began to create her own strategic network.

As a result of that work, she started her practice and in her first year earned around $40,000 to $80,000. But her network helped her to grow her practice and within two years she was generating $800,000.

Just like Sarah did, when you're looking to identify who you need in your 15, look first at the four quadrants Janine talks about.

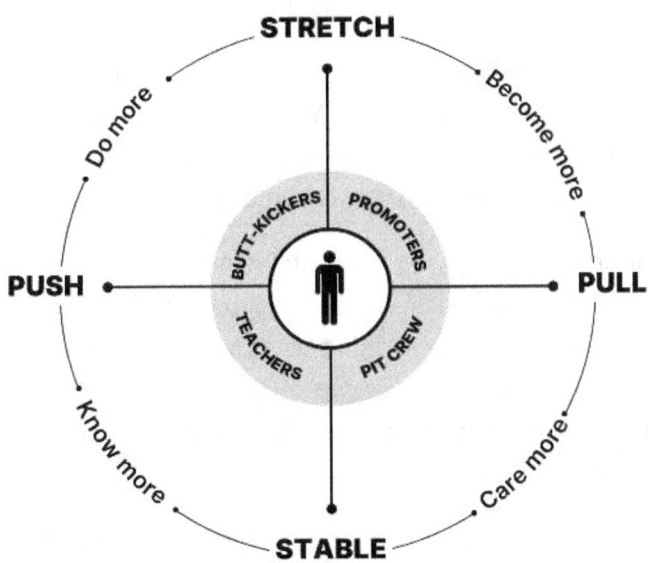

Then ask yourself the following questions:

1. Which of the four types of people from Janine Garner's quadrant do you already have in your 15?
2. Which do you still need?

3. Where are your gaps?
4. What additional elements or traits do you need to feel fully sustainable and supported?

Finding the right mix, with the right additional elements or personality traits, is the key to success in building your strategic network.

Use reminders

Not so long ago, I was trying to get better at building a health routine into my self-care regime. This included things like making sure I drank two litres of water each day, completed my 10,000 steps, took my vitamins, got eight hours sleep – all those things. While these sounded like really obvious things, I was struggling to get them done.

My problem was that I'm really process driven. I like lists. I like checking things off. I like stuff I can get done. And I also work closely with my team to get those things done. To do this I use a system called Asana and my calendar. If it's not in Asana or my calendar, it won't get done.

But I realised that I was trying to remember my self-care routine without these systems. I hadn't taken steps to include these in my calendar or in my Asana task list because I didn't want to clog up my calendar with non-work tasks. But because it was out of sight, out of mind and not visible in my physical workspace where I am all the time, it was simply not getting done.

So I realised that I needed to put it in a place where I was every day to make sure that it was done each day. And that was in my Asana checklist and also in my calendar. And then, these things started getting done each day.

When it comes to self-care, quite often we think it's a separate thing to the systems that we're already using. But if something's working for you in your work routine, think about how you can bring your self-care into those routines. This will ensure that they become a part of how you operate each day. And these reminders will help you embrace your self-care rather than having to remember that there's something outside of work that you need to remember.

Decision fatigue has been shown to impair your ability to make decisions.[15] In fact, when you're struggling with decision fatigue, you also start to take a passive role in your decision making, or could find yourself making impulsive or irrational decisions because you are simply too tired to think it through.[16]

Barack Obama famously wore only grey and navy suits. Steve Jobs had his uniform of jeans, Birkenstocks and turtleneck and Mark Zuckerberg had his plain black shirt or hoodie. They made these choices in order to reduce their own decision fatigue.

Having your reminders and systems in place is like wearing your own 'uniform'. It takes away the need for mental bandwidth around those decisions and will reduce friction and make things a little bit easier both in your business and in your life. Aas Lucille Ball says, 'Love yourself first and everything else falls in line.'

To get started the first thing you need to do is write down the daily tasks that you need to do for your self-care. Put them in your task list and tick them off each day or even block the time in your calendar to make sure they get done. If you need to go to the gym in the morning or in the afternoon, put the time in the calendar to go to the gym. Sounds kind of obvious, but if it's not in there, it more than likely won't happen.

---

[15] Pignatiello, G, Martin, R and Hickman Jr, R. (23 March 2018). 'Decision Fatigue: A Conceptual Analysis'. *Journal of Health Psychology*. Available at https://www.ncbi.nlm.nih.gov/pmc/articles/PMC6119549/.

[16] Pignatiello. Decision Fatigue.

Having a cadence of self-care for sustainability

Your final system is to develop a cadence of self-care. I often think of a cadence of self-care as being a little bit like a treadmill. When the treadmill is set up all you have to do is jump on and get going. You don't have to even think about it.

To create sustainable self-care as a leader, you need to create the habits and routines that make it easy for you to care for yourself. These are what allow your self-care to become sustainable over the long term. If you've got the right habits and routines in place, you reduce decision fatigue and friction in your practice or business, and for you as a leader. You don't even have to think.

By reducing decision fatigue and friction in your self-care, you also reduce the overwhelm. On the other hand, if you don't put these things in place, you'll feel like you come last. You won't be able to prioritise yourself because you'll be too busy responding and reacting to what everybody else needs. And it also ultimately affects your sense of self and your self-esteem.

So we need to put into place the habits for self-care. I love James Clear's book *Atomic Habits*. In it he talks about how the way we spend our time shapes our identity. He says that good habits shape your identity. In other words, your identity emerges from your habits. So the process of building habits is the process of becoming yourself.

I worked for a large productivity company for many years. During that time I worked with a client who said, 'I've got two things I've got to do. The first is that I need to get to the gym each day – I need to get some exercise each day. The second is that I want to read my kids a book before they go to bed every day.'

We said, 'OK, these are habits of self-care and also family care.' The problem with achieving them is that he was being interrupted all the time during his working hours, which made it difficult to meet his goals.

His team were constantly reaching out saying, 'I've got this problem,' or, 'I've got this question. What do I do with this?' And because he was a really nice boss and an empathetic and caring leader, he wanted to help.

So we decided to build in some habits that could create a cadence with his team. In this case that took the form of a daily call, when his team could come to him with questions. So every day at 4pm he would jump online and his team could come to him with their list of questions. The result of this was that the team got all their questions answered, but they also ended up with about a quarter of the amount of questions that they had originally because during the day they'd actually worked out the answers for themselves.

This also meant that my client had most of his day uninterrupted to get on with his work. It meant that he was able to meet his other goals of getting to the gym and reading to his kids every night. And it also meant that he stopped being a crutch for his team by being too available, allowing them to cultivate their own learning and expertise, and build their confidence and skills in the role.

To set up a cadence of self-care for yourself you need to determine what you need to do each day, each week, each month to take care of yourself. For everyone this will look differently. In my case, I have a few really simple things that I do each day. First, I drink two litres of water, I get in my 10,000 steps and I get eight hours sleep. These are tasks that are in my task list that I tick off every day. I put them in my task list because if they're not there, they don't get done because otherwise I have to spend the energy to think about them.

Once you set up your daily self-care tasks, the second thing to think about is what monthly tasks do you do? What self-care might you need on a monthly basis? Maybe you catch up with girlfriends or spend time with extended family. You should also consider what things you do each quarter, and make these part of your quarterly routines.

For me, once a month or sometimes quarterly, I like to have a long weekend away from work. Sometimes I might actually go away, and sometimes I might just take a Friday off to do something for myself. What do you need for yourself monthly and quarterly?

There are other self-care routines you might want to build in. For example, you might like to book in for the dentist every six months or so. And go to a dentist that does reminders for you so you don't have to keep remembering. I go to a dentist specifically for that reason.

Whatever habits that you need to build in to create cadence in your own self-care, that is what you need to do. This will reduce friction and allow you to have sustainability in your care over the long term.

The power of affirmations

When it comes to self-care, never underestimate the power of the unconscious mind. It can serve us so well and help us to create and manifest the life, the career or the business that we want.

Self-affirmations may seem woo woo, but research shows that they help us to access the unconscious mind. By practising self-affirmations we get benefits such as decreased stress, increased wellbeing, improved performance and even become more open to behaviour change.[17] It helps you to remove hesitation and replace it with conviction. It creates an insurance policy around your mindset and negative thinking and allows you to embrace your own self-competence and self-integrity.[18]

I've used positive affirmations with a lot of my clients. One of these was a doctor who was applying for an orthopaedic surgery training program.

---

[17] Cascio, C, O'Donnell, B & et al. 'Self-affirmation activates brain systems associated with self-related processing and reward and is reinforced by future orientation'.

[18] Cascio. Self-affirmation activates brain systems.

He was one of the best doctors I've ever coached and I thought, 'If I ever end up in a hospital and need trauma surgery, God, I hope I get you.'

This doctor also happened to be an Olympic rower. He was incredibly smart and an incredibly high performer. And where some of the other doctors that I was working with thought the power of affirmations were a bit strange. But his background in Olympics training meant that he really understood the power of visualisation, and the power of affirmations for high performance and self-care.

In the lead up to his interview, we did all sorts of things, but a big one that he particularly wanted to work on was his affirmations. His affirmations were things like:

- 'I'm confident.'
- 'I know the answers.'
- 'I'm the best candidate.'

There were lots of different things that we implemented for him to get on to that training program. But the affirmations were something that worked amazingly well. Because of his sporting background, he really understood the power of them to help him with competing on the day. And ultimately he got on the training program he wanted.

I also think about a woman called Sue, who I coach as an expert in communication and leadership skills. She was really trying to grow her business, and in doing that she was doing a lot of things that she'd never done before. We felt we had to create a sense of familiarity and new neural pathways for her growth.

So one particular quarter, we decided to focus on specific affirmations and worked with the unconscious mind to help her to feel a new sense of normal by setting up new neural pathways. It's important to create familiarity so that when we're in uncertainty and change those new neural pathways are where we will default to as opposed to negative thinking. We have to create strong neural pathways, stronger than the previous ones, so that we can move out of fear and into our new normal.

You can think of it like getting out the mower and cutting through long grass and to create a new pathway. It gives us a way to get to our desired space easily and without defaulting to struggling through long grasping grass (or negative thinking).

Louise Hay, who is probably the master of affirmations, has written a number of books on the subject. She says, 'An affirmation opens the door. It's a beginning point on the path to change.' Even Muhammad Ali said it's the repetition of affirmations that leads to belief. Once that belief becomes a deep conviction, things begin to happen.

Affirmations need to become part of your self-care systems. But how do you incorporate them into your life? Ask yourself:

1. What are you wanting to achieve in the next six to 12 months?
2. How do you want to be feeling when you have achieved that? What would be happening?

Now, write down five of those, put them on your bathroom mirror where you'll see them first thing in the morning and last thing at night, and that will help you to reprogram your unconscious mind.

Pay attention to your physical environment

We've all heard of Marie Kondo, the Japanese tidying aficionado. She's famous for saying, 'Tidying your physical space allows you to tend to your psychological space.' Research bears this up, showing that disorganisation and clutter have a cumulative and negative effect on our brains increasing cognitive overload and reducing our working memory..[19]

In other words, your physical environment has an impact on your ability to work. This includes behaviour and performance and even work concentration and productivity.[20]

---

[19] McMains, S & Kastner, S. (12 January 2011). 'Interactions of top-down and bottom-up mechanisms in human visual cortex'. *Journal of Neuroscience*. Available at https://pubmed.ncbi.nlm.nih.gov/21228167/.

[20] Kamarulzaman, N, Saleh, A & et al. (2011). 'An Overview of the Influence of Physical Office Environments towards Employees'. Elsevier Ltd. Presented at The 2nd International Building Control Conference 2011. Available at https://pdf.sciencedirectassets.com/278653/1-s2.0-S1877705811X00164/1-s2.0-S1877705811029730/main.pdf?X-Amz-Security-Token=IQoJb3JpZ2luX2VjENj%2F%2F%2F%2F%2F%2F%2F%2F%2F%2FwEaCX VzLWVhc3QtMSJIMEYCIQDgw4pl5j%2B4HsTm%2B68Byzc2AVIkkawVnwi53OULT CCINAIhAIJsPygQvx3o%2BhiFyJ0ALDfspZYONJYAjZGB9e1%2BpNG0KrsFCIH%2F %2F%2F%2F%2F%2F%2F%2F%2FwEQBRoMMDU5MDAzNTQ2ODY1Igww1T oP5C6eWJgrJh0qjwUwMaKS%2BLorqkxpHEqAkWBFhtXaYWARthNvWlA30SPZur oybULJUpkV1lcs0WGeCsWe%2F14RMyOLIa%2Fd934nSeOTl2h01tU%2FmJDpB %2BOI32XP4fLWGTHfE%2BOMpxAkzhZ7AbC8w76kd1XbpV5O0GzsZTXMtAyTyke 1Pyv2TvLPfRxANEBSoitVHJJtD3shvsUS4%2FWbz%2F6JjGRY3i5fURcE6Wih1Lnm KjZ7cH4dmPl7cfrXrpyGDJSsxStCdri%2BvByOXq%2Ff3Pw4O9I2L1jBeoN5gJRDQ 5VWauiVV7lhp2pWw%2Flt358gJ%2BOYSzhyCvXpubVNdi09WF9Dz7oxRyR%2F% 2FdJdk4vVWncUMz4DQ9%2BMC1ELgNtAFekoBewK1XYeZCEfd5aqNEXZnNr4F74 JLx28ALgkq%2FVPqT9TtpNjMTl5%2FzqZ3gBX038j9tFOItGzEcID%2BRDIISFyksZ ZF%2FsmgeuAIEPpcJsNrn9aJXwSvF3%2BJXV8ZOmauOsimoB4ljh10Zsq9kQXgn SburBR6Rex%2F0pcmO2o6szc0SJYrHoQZKOLO9SyRNz5NMiTNmo67SOle8H1lt N7pQmv5cD0PFxA1nycDf%2FiAVJrufdgCXdNYzcUDbJKOfi0IJGFc5tW45P%2Bwv s8URRPtKYFkSSVI45gdBSOoJngYcTD5hcuFHDJuYDDBJywRhZD6U5hz3%2FOmL 6e8bSdlj84b7b8rnZiWuwS2YW1wMlUnCMbtOdTu5nUEYdrK%2FmVsbbODGCMF YFIPs36SZoCsOsG5K2nm%2FH1Tl2%2BHywX82sFHGkRldXJKIx2puvICC0sQDtpo 7KtZByeU619ehZUpqcK4ywe6bg25S4mc1jn5gomh2678%2Bo%2BQ3AShT7MSX Q9Ykc7MJ6FxqYGOrABn3WbMQLz1UHgJk3Te2seTYdDYL9HL5%2Ba%2BEbSnv8r qSUgLBeryNeZwpCS8SUjIFcfcxm6aDA15SF5w1WNvD7lleHxoj6EJz3SfRwdASEp daMdy%2BteMugNMqpWrHoeCggpN4YB0Hzy%2FZsr4EJJrwj9%2FkY1rAzcNli%2 F6L7dha9yTXnKJ%2FxYpx6pg5p27gw%2B3jvOBnPWjml2DO%2F6%2F5W06uw0

In my own personal experience I've found that when I have a clear physical space that helps me to have a clear mind. I can focus more, am less distracted and think more clearly and creatively. And the research plays this out.

Joanne Love is a Paralympic swim coach and a high-performance expert. She does a lot of work with Olympic swimmers helping them create the high performance they need to be able to win gold medals. In fact, she's written a book called *Gold Medal Goals*. In it she talks about our physical space and physical environment and how we can really make sure that it is in a state that we can work with. Because when we do, we're able to put ourselves into a peak state.[21]

Having a clean work space is kind of like creating a bubble around you. Despite what's going on around you, it allows you to quarantine your space so that you can show up as your best.

To help you set up your physical space, try to get into a routine of cleaning up daily and putting everything in its place so that you can give yourself the space to think. Clear your clutter, put rubbish in the bin, wipe down your surfaces and put things away. Removing all visual clutter will help you have a clear, clean space to work.

DUBqby6Xa62U7u2qhVGFHE4%3D&X-Amz-Algorithm=AWS4-HMAC-SHA256&X-Amz-Date=20230808T002232Z&X-Amz-SignedHeaders=host&X-Amz-Expires=300&X-Amz-Credential=ASIAQ3PHCVTY6IZJIGVN%2F20230808%2Fus-east-1%2Fs3%2Faws4_request&X-Amz-Signature=57e9e05d90b54c1945246af61a25a880dbc52e96ebab11e7857cac9aaee4082e&hash=ca2996bb89ff13db83bb716d5d48cc52d8502ea22859a3e511f80e1237b1fd64&host=68042c943591013ac2b2430a89b270f6af2c76d8dfd086a07176afe7c76c2c61&pii=S1877705811029730&tid=spdf-e24aab51-fd9e-49a7-a818-0b16a2458ff0&sid=3c22886d255c264ecd787056d7cd76f37c42gxrqa&type=client&tsoh=d3d3LnNjaWVuY2VkaXJlY3QuY29t&ua=1b14550651505e07535e&rr=7f339b012fe4a94a&cc=au.

[21] Love, J. (2021). GOLD MEDAL GOALS: The difference between goals that can help and goals that can harm. Proactive Performance Australia.

So often I see people who have worked with and coached thousands of people from desks that were cluttered, scattered and totally unorganised. This was really hindering them, and I believe they were just not able to do their best work, because they weren't really looking after themselves.

They weren't putting their self-care into practice. And their physical space wasn't putting themselves into a state where they could perform at their best. If anything, it was causing them stress. And that's not a great start to being able to care for others.

Conclusion

Making sure that your cup is full is a vital part of running your business – and the only way to have sustainability and success into the future in your practice or business. When your cup is full you are able to really provide both customer and team care – nurturing both – and creating loyal customers and staff.

CHAPTER 5

CUSTOMER CARE

In some ways customer care is the easiest to write about because almost every business is aware of the importance of caring for their customers and clients. There's so much research being done, and so many 'experts' talking about it, that it can be overwhelming. And because of that, it's also one of the most difficult. Particularly when it comes to determining what you really need to do to provide the excellent nurturing and care that your customers deserve.

Just like with self-care, customer or client care encompasses three parts:

1. Mindset
2. Generosity
3. Systems

Let's dive in!

Mindset

Your customer care or client care mindset is the first most important step to nurturing your customers. And this starts with ensuring you always have attention out.

Attention out

What is attention out? Attention out is being aware and mindful of what's happening around you? And it's an important part of taking care of your customers.

Zig Ziglar, the great motivational speaker from the '70s, said, 'You can have everything in life you want, if you will just help other people get what they want.'

This is very true, particularly when it comes to customer care. Instead of it being all about you all the time, you need to be thinking about what your customers and clients want. You are there to serve, support and remove roadblocks. You need to ask the question, 'What do you need?' to every one of your clients and customers. And if you can't reach them individually, then you need to find out this information in some other way.

So often it's easy to fall into the trap of thinking only of your own needs. What are my business needs? And what are my goals? But then it's too easy to become all about me, me, me all the time. So when it comes to nurturing the shift comes when you can look at how others are going?

When it comes to your customers are you noticing what's happening in their lives? If you are able to speak to them directly (like I can in my coaching groups), can you see how their weekend was? How is everything going with their families? What about in their businesses?

If you have a wider customer base, are you listening to your complaints or comments on social media and directly? Are you understanding the problems that your customers are facing?

If you're not, then you need to be. You need to be like a radar, constantly scanning, finding out how they are going, the problems they're facing and the challenges they're talking about. Put on your radar and ask questions, be interested, notice if they look like they're struggling and find out how they're going. It's about being interested and listening and asking questions.

A few years ago, I won something called the Attention Out Award, which was awarded in a community I was in. I won this award simply because I was paying attention to my clients and my team. What I was doing was being available so that I could talk to people and ask them questions. I asked them what help they needed and tried to find out how they're going. I asked, 'What's been the best thing that's happened in your practice over the last quarter? Where are your wins? What are you working on at the moment?'

If you're worried that you're focusing too much on yourself, or on your own business, ask yourself:

1. What are you noticing about your clients or customers?
2. How often do you check in? If you work face-to-face with clients, then you can do this often. Otherwise you might need to reach out via an email or phone call or even through your email comms or social media.
3. How often do you ask them if they're OK? How often do you follow up on something? And how much time do you have allocated for follow ups or one-on-ones (if that's possible in your business model)?
4. What can you do to build more attention out into your practice?

Customer for life

Jay Abraham, founder and CEO of The Abraham Group, Inc., says that there are three things needed to increase your business – increase the number of clients, increase the average size of the sale per client and increase the number of times clients return and buy again. And while we often talk about getting more clients, or price increases, we don't often focus on how to keep a customer for life.

Keeping a customer for life is a vital part of building your business. And creating a culture of care in your business is a vital part of creating a customer for life. We do that by treating customers as if they are going to be in your business and in your life for a very long time.

Benefits of increasing your customer lifetime value

When you are trying to find new clients all the time, it eats into your costs and increases your churn rate. That's because customer acquisition costs a great deal more than customer retention. But if you want less costs and churn, you need to really have a mindset that you're going to have this customer for life. And once you do that, then you're in a position to set up your culture, your systems and your practice around clients that are going to be around for a long time.

Robbie Kellman Baxter, who wrote The Forever Transaction, says, 'By treating your customers like members, and focusing on helping them achieve their desired ongoing outcome (forever promise) you will build deeper relationships, increase customer lifetime value and probably enjoy more predictable revenue.'

Of course, some people may not want as much intimacy in their business or practice. And in that case, having high customer turnover can suit them. However, for most of us, customer churn is not a great way to build up our businesses or practices. And it's not a great way to deliver extraordinary customer service to our clients either.

Creating a forever customer

Recently I had the good fortune to be able to coach a client who's just started working with me again. I coached her about five years ago and through a different program. And recently she came back to me and said, 'I'd love to do some more work with you.'

Of course, this wasn't out of the blue. Since we'd last worked together, we'd stayed friends. I'd continued to have a relationship with her, and we always stayed connected. We often would run into each other at events, and I'd often touch base just to say hi.

When she came back to work with me, I continued to build our relationship because the work it takes to build a lifelong client doesn't end when they start to pay you. That's not the end result, and that's simply not enough.

As part of our work together my client joined a retreat and a boot camp that I was running. She brought her husband along, not to participate, but just to have a little holiday. When I heard that he was there at the hotel I said, 'Why doesn't he come to dinner and join us for lunch? Considering he's there, that's fine.'

They both really appreciated the fact that her husband could join in, despite not having paid for the boot camp. But when you're building lifetime customers (or increasing customer lifetime value) it's important to think about what the clients want and need, and look beyond just 'what they've paid for'. Instead we need to think of our clients like family and commit to looking after them like family. That's the way to build customers for life.

Involving my client's husband was particularly important in this case because he is in her top 15. He is one of her primary supporters and has a big influence on her success.

Increasing the lifetime value of one customer to impact others

One of the things that my lovely client asked me when we were on our retreat was if there was anybody there that she could talk to for me. She said, 'There are some people in this group that I think might be a good fit for you. Do you want me to answer any questions for anyone? Or is there anyone that I could have a chat with to support you?'

This was both exceptionally kind and a great example of how putting in the energy to increase the lifetime value of one customer can leverage your ability to impact many. For her, the focus had shifted from a 'pay for what you get' relationship, to a relationship of care and reciprocity. In fact, she actually sent me a beautiful gift after the event saying, 'Thank you so much for being so inclusive of my husband and making him feel so welcome.'

So, when you're building a lifetime customer mindset you have to remember that it's not just about business. It's about what is going to improve the life of this person. And the more you're able to do that, the more your customers and clients will talk to others about you allowing your impact to spread.

Creating habits that build lifetime customers

Building lifetime customers is a mindset. You might think that this just comes naturally to me. It is true that I am naturally inclined to put a lot of care into my work and my relationships. But the processes that I have in place to accomplish this are all things I learned from people that I worked with in business. And that means that anyone can learn them too. If you can create habits, then you'll adopt it as part of your DNA.

Building habits that create a lifetime customer is really about being clear about who your ideal customers are. And once you find them, it's about treating them like a family member. But to do that you've got to really look at what is happening for this person and how you can make it better for them.

Ask yourself:

1. What is happening for your client?
2. Why are they working with you?
3. What steps can you take when your initial work together is finished?
4. What steps can you take if they don't continue working with you?
5. What do they say after you're finished working together?

6. How can you stay connected?
7. Have they become an advocate for you?

The power of insights

One of the best ways to nurture your clients is to ask yourself, 'what does my client need in order to grow?' Once you determine their needs, then you ask yourself, 'what insights do I have to help make that happen?'

Henry Ford is famous for saying, 'If I had asked people what they wanted, they would have said faster horses.' And that's because though his customers knew the problems they were facing, they didn't have the insights for the best solutions. But Henry Ford did.

Ford's vision, innovation and creativity meant he anticipated what people needed next. If asked, they would have said 'faster horses' because they couldn't imagine that cars – with all their potential for faster and further travel – could exist.

Ford took it to the next level with his insights.

Nurture is the result of insights + challenge

Insights are only the first step to nurturing clients. In order to truly nurture, we need to know when to use our insights in order to challenge the status quo. It's in the challenge that individuals experience growth.

A great example of someone who both nurtures and challenges is matchmaker Aleeza Ben Shalom – otherwise known as 'the Jewish matchmaker' from the Netflix series of the same name.

If you haven't seen it, when Aleeza meets a new client, she first asks what they are seeking in a partner. This can include their looks, their lifestyle and even their level of religious dedication. Aleeza then considers what each client needs and makes thoughtful matches for them.

She has had a lot of success. And part of what makes her so successful is that she isn't afraid to challenge her clients with her insights.

For example, Aleeza met with one client who claimed to want to meet a partner with blue eyes and supermodel good looks. As she worked with him it was clear that he was perhaps focusing on the wrong things.

But Aleeza was nurturing and kind, waiting until she'd listened to everything he had to say before gently asking him if she could give him a bit of dating advice. Because of her warmth, and his trust in her experience, her client was open to her suggestions and experienced some growth because of it.

In this way, the Jewish Matchmaker gives her clients insight from her experience, and delivers it in a way that is acceptable to her client. She gently challenges her clients' expectations of a potential partner, using her insights and experience to find a partner most holistically suited to them, with great success.

Know when to challenge

A great example of nurturing is in the international bestseller by Matthew Dixon and Brent Adamson, *The Challenger Sale: How to take control of the customer conversation*. In it the authors argue that the key to sales success is not just to build and maintain relationships with customers but to challenge them.

The *Challenger Sale* shows us that the key to nurturing clients is to approach them with insights tailored to their specific needs. It's essential to be assertive, questioning and push back where necessary, rather than just providing the customer with what they've asked for. It's only this way that they can experience growth and improvement.

High performance vs core performance

In writing *The Challenger Sale*, the authors assessed the Five Profiles of Sales Professionals:

Hard Worker	Challenger	Relationship-Builder	Lone Wolf	Problem Solver
• Goes the extra mile • Interested in feedback & development • Self-motivated	• Understands the customer's business • Pushes the customer • Has a different worldview • Loves to debate	• Gets along with everyone • Generous in giving time to help others • Builds strong customer advocates	• Self-assured • Independent • Follows own instincts	• Ensures that all problems are solved • Details-oriented • Reliably responds

In analysing the different types of sales professionals, the authors looked at high sales performers vs core sales performers. The Challengers outperformed the Relationship Builders because they tailored their response and asserted control in the customer relationship. Their research found that on average, nearly 40% of high performers were Challengers. But in complex sales situations, 54% of high performers are Challengers.

Though Relationship Builders are successful and have important personal and professional attributes, they are limited in a complex sales situation. According to The Challenger Sale, Challenger sales reps use their understanding of their customers' businesses to bring new ideas that the customer hadn't previously considered or realised. They can deliver new insights and drive thinking in innovative ways.

And because of that they are able to nurture their customers' growth – either by helping them save money, avoid risk, grow their business or develop individually. In other words, it's the Challengers' insights that help nurture a client's growth.

In my own practice I've seen how insights and challenging lead to nurturing growth. And it's an important focus for me for each and every one of my clients.

1. When you're looking to adopt a nurturing, challenger mindset, you can start by asking yourself:
2. What do you feel like you want to say to people but are too scared to say it?
3. This could be the insight they need to make the important growth they want.

Have a lucky mindset

When you have a lucky mindset, you radiate positivity and possibility, you attract opportunities, the right clients and the right staff. People start to come around you.

Four things that lucky people do differently, based on the research from Dr Richard Wiseman's book, *The Luck Factor: The Scientific Study of the Lucky Mind*, are:

1. They expose themselves to a wide variety of networks and experiences.
2. They expect to be lucky.
3. They find the good in anything.[1]
4. They listen to their own lucky hunches.

If you don't have a lucky mindset, you'll find yourself with a scarcity mindset. And this will lead to a 'woe is me', feeling, and problems, issues, dramas and challenges. And that will just repel people. People simply don't want to be around those kinds of issues. They want to be

---

[1] Wiseman, R. (2011). The Luck Factor: The Scientific Study of the Lucky Mind. Cornerstone Digital.

people who are high-vibing. They want to be around people who make them feel good.

In *The Luck Factor*, Dr Wiseman discusses the research that they did with students that were walking between two classrooms. In that study, they planted $50 notes on the grounds that the students were walking through. They found that of those students that were walking, those who had a lucky mindset were far more likely to see the $50 note than those that didn't have a lucky mindset. The belief they were lucky actually meant they were lucky.[2]

Years ago, I had a staff member who was an area manager in a retail store. One day I asked her, 'How are you going?' She said, 'It's just so quiet. It's so dead. We're just not getting any customers in.' So I asked her, 'Have you acknowledged those two customers over there?' And she said, 'Oh, no. I will. But yeah, it's just been really quiet.'

This area manager was so busy talking about the doom and gloom, and how many problems, issues, dramas, challenges the shop had, she didn't even see the customers that she already had. Her energy was like, 'I don't really want to help.' And so that doesn't make people really feel like they want to be in the store. She was so worried about being unlucky that she couldn't see the lucky opportunities right in front of her.

It's the same thing for you as a leader. Do you have a lucky mindset? Are you able to focus on the opportunities and clients you already have? Or are you too focused on the negative?

A person who is really great at this is Emma McQuee, a business coach based in Melbourne. I call her Pollyanna because she is always seeing the silver lining and truly has a lucky mindset. With Emma every day's a great day. And she's someone that her clients really want to be around.

---

[2] Wiseman. The Luck Factor.

So my question to you is, on a scale of one to 10, how lucky do you think you are? And how much of that mindset affects your luck, opportunities and possibilities. How much of it impacts your ability to notice the things that are right in front of you?

Making care your north star

Before the era of satellite navigation, sailors used to navigate by using the stars. And due to its consistent position in the sky, they'd often use the north star as a navigational tool. They could accurately determine their ships latitude by measuring the angle between the northern horizon and the north star and by its guiding light, navigate their way home.

In the same way, if you're serious about making care your core value and competitive advantage, you really need to make it like your north star. When care is your north star it becomes the key value that helps you make decisions when you're feeling unclear or lost in the dark.

In order to start making care your north star for your customers you always need to be asking yourself, what is the nurturing thing to do?

Your customers have fears – fear that they're going to make a mistake, that they're going to stuff something up, that they're going to do the wrong thing and that they're going to somehow lose their business.

When you ask yourself what is the nurturing thing to do, you're really asking, 'How can I help?' How do I fix this problem? And how do I help to make sure it doesn't happen again? If you can answer those then you're going to be able to make sure that everybody is served, not just the client.

One of the things that I've done in my practice to make care my north star is to incorporate it into our team charter. And one of the things the team charter covers is travelling safety. So, if anyone's travelling, which is usually me, we always have someone meet that person. This is especially important if we're travelling at night, or in a foreign country. But it also matters even if one of us is just going one state over. We make sure that there's someone meeting them to help them and guide them so they're never alone.

Margaret Mead, who is the great anthropologist, was the person who first made the connection between broken bones and care. She discovered in her archeological digs a healed human femur. She posited that this showed that the individual had been nursed back to health and cared for while recovering from fractures. For her this was the first evidence of true civilised society, because it was the first evidence of care for another. [3]

Margaret Mead also said, 'Never doubt that a small group of thoughtful committed individuals can change the world. In fact, it's the only thing that ever has.'

Embrace values driven leadership

I had a team member whose father passed away and his mother became unwell in the same week. It was a really terrible situation. At the same time, things at work were quite hectic, and we desperately needed him on point. But we also knew that the caring thing to do was to just step up and make sure that he had the space to go and deal with what was happening in his life. So that's what we did.

So we got our team together. I put in a lot of extra hours and covered for him with a client that he'd been working with. I certainly wasn't the best executive assistant for this client, but she really appreciated that I was stepping in. At the same time, the rest of my team stepped in behind me so that we could better support this person. And in the end the work

---

[3] Lasco, G. (16 June 2022). 'Did Margaret Mead Think a Healed Femur Was the Earliest Sign of Civilization?' Sapiens.org. Available at https://www.sapiens.org/culture/margaret-mead-femur/.

gets done and people understand. Even better, the result was a happy and loyal client, and a happier and more loyal team as well.

Values really drive growth. And as a leader in your business and with your customers, you will realise your full potential when the values you espouse are embraced by your full organisation and team. Research shows that the results are an 'authentic and sustainable business culture.'[4]

So how do you create value-driven leadership with your customers? Ask yourself, how congruent does care feel to you? Does it feel like you're just doing it because you want to say that you want to be caring? Or do you actually believe it? Are there other ways that you demonstrate this and are you known for it? Is your organisation known for it?

If you're wanting to change that narrative, then you've really got to look at not just putting some values on a wall, but it has to be embedded in every part of our organisation. Every member of your team needs to demonstrate it for your customers and create more opportunities for values driven care.

Always get the dog's name

Digital marketing pioneer and *Wall Street Journal* best-selling author Ann Handley set out a fantastic list of 40 time-tested tips that never go out of style. While it's aimed at journalists, the tip taking out the #1 spot is applicable to all of us who want to learn how to be better consultants: always get the name of the dog.[5]

But what does this mean?

---

[4] 'Values-Driven Leadership Framework.' Benedictine University. Available at https://cvdl.ben.edu/leadership-framework/.

[5] Handley, A. '40 time-tested tips that never go out of style'. @here for the journalism. Poynter. Available at https://poyntercdn.blob.core.windows.net/files/40jtips.pdf.

Well, the idea is that if you manage to get all of your client's personal details down pat, even down to the name of their dog, then you know enough about your client. When you know the name of the dog you should also be able to answer whether they are married, have children, where they live and, of course, do they have pets.

Why does this matter? Well knowing your customer is one of the most important steps to providing real customer care.

Business leader, speaker and seven-time *New York Times* best-selling author Harvey Mackay has spent many decades touting his golden rule of selling. And not surprisingly it is, *know your customer*.[6] He believes that having an established relationship with the person you're selling to is crucial in business.

In fact, Harvey believes so strongly in knowing your client that he developed The Mackay 66 Customer Profile.[7] This is a report that outlines the 66 things you should know about every client you work with. It covers everything from their sports interests and favourite place for lunch to their personal goals.

Once again, it's not about prying but a way of encouraging you to talk more deeply with them and helping you get to know them over time. This is so crucial in your learning how to be a better consultant.

---

[6] Mackay, H. (26 November 2010). 'The Golden Rule of selling: Getting to know your customers'. Tampa Bay Business Journal. Available at https://www.bizjournals.com/tampabay/print-edition/2010/11/26/the-golden-rule-of-selling.html.

[7] The Mackay 66 Customer Profile. [Template]. Harvey Mackay Academy. Available at https://members.harveymackayacademy.com/wp-content/uploads/2018/12/Mackay-66_Updated-2018.pdf.

Nurture Your Existing Clients

As Richard Branson once said, when it comes to nurturing your customers, the key is to 'set realistic expectations and then exceed them, preferably in helpful and unexpected ways'.

Too often consultants single-mindedly chase new sales opportunities, and in the process lose sight of the clients they currently serve. We all know that sales are crucial to business, but have you stopped to think about who the people are that you need to be selling to and how you can remain connected to them after they have bought from you?

There are three types of sales meetings you should be having each week to help increase your revenue growth.

1. Meeting 1. Your Top 150s Meeting – this is about keeping connected to your existing customer base.
2. Meeting 2. Database Meeting – this is finding out who the top openers of your communications are and finding a way to help them.
3. Meeting 3. Creative Sales Meetings – this is brainstorming as a team to find ways to connect, build relationships and solve problems.

Systems are key

When you have a small business you can pretty easily keep on top of your clients. But once your business grows , it becomes much harder to know everyone in the same way.

This is where good systems come in.

When dealing with a lot of clients, you need to be able to make notes and keep them on file for when you need them. As Harvey Mackay says regarding the Mackay 66, you need to guard this information and be sensitive to how you use it and who has access.

If you want to know your customers better, follow these steps:

1. Take a look at your top 150 customers.
2. Pinpoint those that you don't know well enough.
3. Then determine what you need to do to get to know them better.
4. Finally, make that happen!

Generosity

Now that you understand the elements that go into your customer care mindset, it's time to think about the next part of the process. And that is embracing generosity.

Being generous to your customers is not about giving them free products or services. But it is about having a generous spirit and generously giving them the things that will help them to grow and develop both as people and in their own businesses.

Charge well so you can care more

The first thing you need to consider when trying to be more generous is your pricing. Premium prices allow you to be generous. In other words, when you are priced correctly you have the freedom to be generous. You have that flexibility built in because you know that you know that you're already being valued.

On the other hand, when you aren't priced properly then you might get resentful. You'll start trying to scrabble back those additional amounts through your services. You'll fret over any additional work that your client might ask for, and rigidly stick to the scope of work. And that will stop you from being truly generous in your practice.

In order to be generous, you need to review your pricing. I know this can be confronting, so sometimes it works best to talk to someone else you trust. Get outside information about what the going rates are in your industry and consider how you might increase your pricing – either across the board or for certain products or services. In this way you'll be setting yourself up for a generous practice or business.

Provide exceptional value

I worked with a client, Mel, who was really trying to grow her business. The challenge was that her prices were too cheap. But she was afraid to raise her prices.

The issue wasn't with her pricing, however. The real issue was that she didn't have a strong value proposition. She hadn't really thought about how she could create value for her clients and how that would help them to buy.

A great value proposition demonstrates what you, as a brand, have to offer to your customers. This is something that no other competitor has or a service or product that fulfils a need that no other company is able to fill. But most importantly it's customer-focused and demonstrates that you understand your customers' experiences or challenges.[8] This is essentially generosity.

So, generosity involves providing exceptional value to your customers. When you provide exceptional value, it shows that you've really thought about the challenges your customers are facing and the tools and things that they need to help them succeed. It shows that you've paid attention to their needs and have the empathy to really find the solutions they need. It also shows the depth of insight and understanding that you have about the problem that they've got.

---

[8] Customer Lifecycle, LLC. Value Proposition Development. Green Book Directory. Available at https://www.greenbook.org/marketing-research/value-proposition-development-34754.

When you provide exceptional value you become a no-brainer to work with. Your clients can see that they're not just signing up to an expensive nothing. They recognise that you're not trying to rip them off or screw them over. The value you provide proves to them that you really do care and that you really do want to help.

Albert Einstein once said, 'Strive not to be a success, but rather to be of value.'

If you're trying to grow you'll want to show that you can care and nurture and look after your clients. And to do that you'll want to look at the current value offer that you have for them. So, ask yourself:

- Is this good value?
- Would you buy it?
- Is there a strong value proposition?
- Would your customers get a good return?
- Are they actually buying? What are your current close rates? If it's over 50%, then they are buying. But if it's moving closer to zero, then they're not buying.
- If they're not buying, how can you increase the value? What creative ideas have you got that could really help support the growth for this client and therefore help you to grow your own business?

Ban the 'waiting' word

When you're creating a culture of care in your practice or business, there's one word that should be banned completely. Waiting. Instead you need to remember that the ball is in your court and it's always in your court.

The 'waiting' word is something that you never want to hear (and certainly not say!) in your work. This is where someone on your staff might say, 'I'm waiting to hear back from….' Or 'I'm waiting to touch base until....' Or where you might even say to yourself, 'I'm waiting for a better time to....'

But when you're building a culture of care – when you're truly looking to nurture your clients and customers, then 'waiting' is almost never the right response.

When you're 'waiting' for something, you have essentially lost your power and your control. You aren't taking steps, you aren't initiating actions and you have no influence. You're just stuck sitting on your hands waiting for someone else to take steps or initiate action. You're waiting for that other person to influence the outcomes whether or not this is waiting for information or waiting for the right conditions.

This is not a great position to be in, in your practice.

Impacts of 'waiting'

When you're sitting on your hands waiting, you can experience some negative impacts.These can include:

1. Lack of control
2. Lack of influence
3. Lost opportunities (opportunity cost)
4. Time and energy wasted
5. Culture of care undermined

Taking action

Instead of 'waiting' you could be taking action. If you're waiting for information, go out and get it. Poll your audience. Talk to your community. Research or study if necessary. If the information exists, there are ways to access it.

If you're waiting for someone to get back to you, take action by scheduling your next point of contact. Rather than 'I'm waiting for him to get back to me,' this becomes, 'I will reach out again on Wednesday morning.' This allows you to clear it from your mind, because you know that something is in the schedule. In the meantime you're now open to work on something else, rather than wasting your time and energy focused on something you had no control over.

The ball is in your court

Seth Godin says, 'When someone does care enough (about you, about the opportunity, about the work or the tool), the ball is in your court'. This is how you create a culture of care through action. It's important to remember that the ball is in your court, and, importantly, it's always in your court. It's your job to reach out. It's your job to gather information. It's your job to take action.

Impacts of action

When you take action you get some excellent results. You will:

- Regain control
- Retain influence
- Open up opportunities
- Focus your time and energies effectively
- Create a culture of care

How action creates a culture of care

Care is a vital part of running an exceptional and successful business or practice. A culture of care leads to strong positioning and loyal clients and customers, while also reducing your need to continually reach out to new clients. And because of that it becomes your competitive advantage.

There's a wonderful consultant in my community called Amy. Amy had excellent sales results in the last quarter. But she'd had a few tough quarters previous to that one. I had always been concerned about the support she had around her, feeling that it wasn't enough. So I sat down with her and suggested that if she had the right support she could free up more capacity.

Amy's response was very typical, and understandable. She wanted to wait until she was more certain of her cash flow. In other words, she was 'waiting' for something else (mostly out of her control) to happen.

I felt that waiting was definitely not the right answer for Amy. It was disempowering and it was tying up her ability to make real changes in her business. She was stuck in a holding pattern. So I suggested that she just get started by hiring someone for five or 10 hours a week. But she still felt that it was beyond her.

So I designed an online course on how to hire a rockstar VA. This included all the knowledge that I'd gained running my own business and hiring my own team. This included the right questions to ask, how to do job ads and what to look for in your own team. With this information in her back pocket Amy felt empowered to find her own VA.

When I took action (by designing the course for hiring a VA) I was demonstrating my own culture of care. And now that Amy has the support that she needs, she's able to share that care with her own clients.

Culture of Care Model

Stephen Covey created his circle of concern and circle of influence model, which distinguishes between proactive people and reactive people.[9] Of course, as leaders we are striving to be proactive rather than reactive. And the model helps us to see how to get there.

---

[9] 'Stephen Covey's circle of concern and circle of influence.' Development Partnership. Available at https://dplearningzone.the-dp.co.uk/wp-content/uploads/sites/2/2015/06/Covey.pdf.

Covey's Circles of Influence

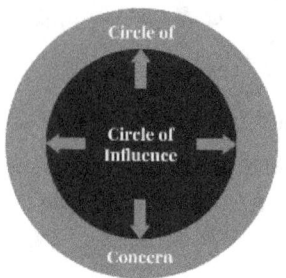
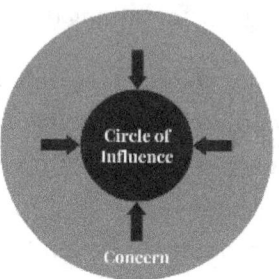

Proactive Focus
Positive energy enlarges Circle of Influence

Reactive Focus
Negative energy reduces Circle of Influence

Source: DP Learning Zone[10]

In this model we have the things we care about which are represented by the bigger circle. These might be crime in your suburb, the curriculum at your child's school, your fitness and your family's nutritional needs (for example). The smaller circle contains those things that are actually in your circle of influence. This pulls in the things that you care about but that you also have some control over. In this case, it likely includes your fitness and your family's nutritional needs.

When it comes to building a culture of care, I want to add one more inner circle. This circle is your circle of care.

---

[10] Stephen Covey's circle of concern and circle of influence.

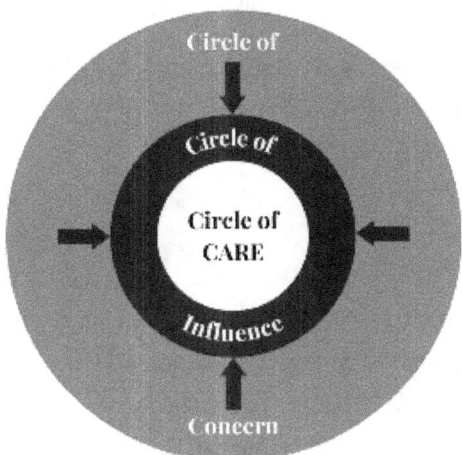

Within the circle of care are the things that you care about but that you also choose to do something about. Maybe today that doesn't include your fitness, but it does include meeting your family's nutritional needs, for example. For most of us, we'll have many things in our circle of care – and many things that we're taking action on, both in our personal lives and in our work. But building in the processes and systems that allow us to expand our inner circle of care will help us create that overall culture of care.

Banning the waiting word is one of those ways that we can expand our circle of care. Each time we schedule a time to reach out to a client, or build in a process that helps us raise our capacity and take action, we banish waiting and build in opportunities for care.

Getting started

To get started, ask yourself the following questions:

1. What care are you currently giving your clients?
2. Are you able to banish the 'waiting' word from your own business or practice?
3. How will you do that?

Stay connected

Being connected with your customers is one of the best ways to stay generous with them. When you are connected with your customers, it's a little bit like being a magnet. You stay magnetised to people so that you can make sure that they're nurtured and looked after so that they can grow. And when you're connected you're able to find those opportunities to be generous and giving.

However, I've also found that this is one of the areas that many leaders struggle with. They don't know how to connect – or they worry about the costs of both their time and resources. But staying connected doesn't have to take up a lot of time or really even cost money. All it takes is getting outside of yourself and being interested in others – in this case your clients and customers. It's about sending texts, cards, emails and maybe even sometimes gifts. It's about thinking about what they need and helping them out when you can.

People are lonely, lost, and disconnected and the fact that you've taken the time to both notice what they need and help them makes them feel like they belong. And this can add so much value to their lives and work because, frankly, most just don't generally receive this kind of care.

I receive many beautiful gifts and cards. My husband often comes home and says, 'Far out. You get a lot of stuff.' I don't expect a lot of things, but it is really nice to be thought about and cared for. To be honest, however, one of the main reasons that this occurs is because I send a lot of things out too. I love for people to be acknowledged. I want to thank them and be generous, and to be able to show that 'I'm interested in you. I care for you. I want you to know that I want to help you and I'm really enjoying being part of your business and helping you.' And sending a card, flowers or a small thoughtful gift does that.

I was working with a client recently and I asked them to introduce this kind of system into their work. So they picked out a client they'd done some work with many years ago, but hadn't been in touch with for some time.

I challenged my client to get back on the phone with them because I was aware that the organisation was going through a lot of change at that time and over the last few years. And we also knew that they liked world-class providers. They liked the best of the best. Which my client was. They were in a position to help their clients through this challenging time with world class solutions.

So my client reached out, and, as a result, they said, 'Oh my God, yes, please come and work with us. We're running this event and need help.' They spent $20,000 that day. On top of that, they then invited my client to some of their VIP and private 'invite only' events, and went on to spend another $200,000 that year.

So while you can sit back and 'wait for people to buy me', the reality is that people will reward your attention and support and spend a lot more now and into the future when you take proactive steps to connect.

Of course, when it comes to connection – true connection – you've got to do it genuinely. Your clients have to know that the desire for connection comes from a place of enjoying working with them and wanting to do more of that. If you don't like working with them, it's going to come across as a bit inauthentic.

I had a client who was in the media quite a bit. I'd watch TV, and when I'd see him on the TV show, I'd send him a note and say, 'Congratulations.

Well done. Awesome job on TV tonight. Loved that you said this. I think that really resonated.' That built a connection between us, even more so because I genuinely meant everything that I said. But it was because of that connection that he stayed with me for a long time. In fact, he's still a customer today.

As Brené Brown says, 'Connection is why we're here. It's why we have purpose and meaning in our lives.'

So the questions become which of your customers do you most want to work with? What creative ideas do you have to help stay connected with them? Remember that these don't always have to be paid things. Maybe it's a phone call or a test message, a card or a small gift.

You could also organise a shared experience? You can work with charities or get involved with a charity event and invite your clients. This is a great idea, particularly if you know the charities and causes that matter to your community. But whatever you do, make sure it helps you to create a sense of belonging, meaning and purpose by nurturing and staying connected and helping them achieve their potential.

The power of empathy

Empathy is an important part of customer care. And it overarches everything else we've spoken about so far, including connection. But most importantly, empathy is what sets great leaders apart. Empathy is the glue that holds the people you are leading together.

So what is an empathetic leader? Well, empathic leaders show genuine concern and care for their customers and clients, whether it's about their emotional health or the challenges they're facing in work and business. It's easy to start by just asking about their lives so you can understand their struggles, become aware of their feelings and thoughts and offer the right kind of support and help.

Dr Daniel Goleman, psychologist and leading researcher on empathy, says that leaders with empathy do more than just sympathise with people.[11] They use their knowledge to improve their customers and clients in subtle and important ways. And they help them to continuously improve and find ways to grow and improve.[12]

The research also tells us that empathy is one of the top competitive advantages and required skills to be an effective leader.[13] When I was the head of capability for an organisation, I had a team member, Lisa. I was responsible for increasing the capabilities at our retail stores, and I really wanted Lisa on the team because she'd spent a lot of time working at the store and knew how to get her store to perform really well.

But Lisa was also heavily tattooed and pretty gruff when she spoke. Because of that I had pressure from some of the senior team to keep her at the retail level, rather than promoting her to a managerial position. They believed she wasn't really executive material or to the standard that they expected simply because of the way she appeared outwardly.

Most of the senior team, however, had come out of finance and banking and had strong white collar backgrounds. On the other hand, a lot of the people who had worked in the retail side of the business were very blue collar. They related to Lisa and because of that felt comfortable to rally behind her. But what I loved most about Lisa was that because of her

---

[11] Goleman, D. (2004). 'What Makes a Leader?' *Harvard Business Review.* Available at https://hbr.org/2004/01/what-makes-a-leader.

[12] Goleman. What Makes a Leader?

[13] Zivkovic, S. (April 2022). 'Empathy in Leadership: How it Enhances Effectiveness'. [Conference address.] Presented at the 80th International Scientific Conference on Economic and Social Development and 10th International OFEL Conference "Diversity, Equity and Inclusion: The Essence of Organisational Well-Being" at: Dubrovnik, Croatia. Available at https://www.researchgate.net/publication/361952690_Empathy_in_Leadership_How_it_Enhances_Effectiveness.

work on the shop floor she brought the competitive advantage of empathy.

Lisa really knew what the store managers were going through. She knew what the team members were going through. She knew what the customers were going through. And she had the empathy to understand the dynamics that impacted each of them. And that empathy for the customers and the store managers was key to us helping us to create programs that led to a 50% decrease in turnover in around 100 stores.

So having empathy is really about having the understanding, insight and care, and the skills to use those when you need it, in order to understand your customer really well. But the first step in doing this, in becoming an empathic leader, is to be curious. It's not about prying, but it's being genuinely curious about their life, what they do outside of work and the challenges they experience. Secondly it's about being interested. You need to be open to their ideas and experiences. Even if they have a different skillset or different background than you.

Lisa had a different background to the senior team, and even a different background to me (despite the fact that we both came from retail shop floors). But by accepting and respecting other people's expertise your team and your customers will ultimately benefit. And that's because they have empathy in ways that you may not.

Systems

The final step in customer care is the same as self-care, and that is to have the systems in place to support your customer care mindset and generous approach. There are many systems that people will sell to you (from workflow software to calendar systems) and these are of course important. But you also need to have those unique systems that overarch your customer care generally and relate to your specific set of clients or customers.

Stay in touch

Staying in touch is the system that relates to connection, attention out and more. And it involves setting up the processes within your business that allows you to stay in touch with your customers and clients in a genuine and authentic way. This is not about selling anything – it's about being interested.

When we have the processes in place to stay in touch, it can help our customers feel they're really valued and that you're nurturing them and looking after them. If we only reach out to sell, then people can feel like a commodity. They'll suspect we're only in it for ourselves.

So how do we stay in touch?

First, you have to have a process for identifying your top clients and customers. Those you love to work with. But quite often when I ask people, particularly business owners, 'Who do you lead?', they'll often say, 'I've only got my assistant.' They fail to realise that you are not only a leader to your team, you're also a leader for your customers and clients.

So start by identifying the top thousand people who you lead, and work out how you're going to stay in touch with them. Then make an additional plan for your top 100 customers (those that you love working with) and implement that. In this way you'll be able to stay in touch.

I worked with a client, Lockey, who was a senior manager for a property company. Years previously I had worked with him on updating his resume and his LinkedIn profile which had helped him get the job at his current company.

As part of my routine with him, I had kept in touch, checking in regularly to find out how he was travelling and how things were going in his new job. One time when I checked he replied with his usual, 'It's going great,' but then followed that up by saying, 'Actually, I wanted to talk to you. I've been thinking about getting a speaker for an event and I thought of you. They normally use celebrity speakers, but I'd love to see if maybe I could get you in because I think what you can help us with would be really valuable.'

He wanted something more practical for the team, while still being both inspiring and educational. So I got in there, delivered the keynote, and then was contracted to work with the organisation for 12 months to help them to develop their marketing strategy and focus on their growth. And that wouldn't have happened if I hadn't reached out to say hello and see how he is going.

The research tells us that it takes about eight touch points to convert a customer.[14] But the research is also telling us that these touchpoints are expanding – and customers are requiring more to get to the same place – with new companies providing anywhere from 20 to 500 touchpoints.[15] This is partly because it's getting less expensive to utilise touchpoint-centred engagement, partly because critical capabilities are easier to access and partly because next-generation engagement continues to soar.[16] In other words, it's getting easier to reach out, more difficult to be heard and tech is complicating both.

You might notice this in your online shopping. You might look at a pair of shoes on a website like Jimmy Choo and then the next thing you

---

[14] Schultz, M. (29 March 2023). 'How Many Touches Does It Take to Make a Sale?' Rain Group. Available at https://www.rainsalestraining.com/blog/how-many-touches-does-it-take-to-make-a-sale#:~:text=The%20simple%20answer%20is%3A%20more,conversion)%20with%20a%20new%20prospect.

[15] Tordjman, K, Poddar, B & Philippon, A. (21 February 2023). 'Touchpoints and the Revolution in Omnichannel'. Boston Consulting Group. Available at https://www.bcg.com/publications/2023/touchpoints-and-omnichannel-revolution.

[16] Tordjman. Touchpoints and the Revolution in Omnichannel.

know, you're getting ads about those shoes (and similar) following you around everywhere. And that's because of the 20 touch points.

Years ago I connected with a real estate agent who I had bought a house from years ago. The house was an investment property in a country town – a place where I didn't even live. But every quarter I would hear from him. He would say, 'Good day, Jane. How you going? Just ringing to see how the house is going. Hope you have a great Easter. See you.'

Every quarter he'd ring to say, good day. We'd have a little chat, or he'd leave a message. That's all he did. But it did make him memorable. And even though I might not be selling a property in his area, at some stage I knew someone who was – and I was more than happy to refer them.

So when did you last reach out to your customers, not to sell something, but just to say good day? Just to check in how they're going? When was the last time you sent them something – a text, a card or even an email? What else can you do to stay in touch?

And how can you create systems to support your ability to reach out? Can you create an onboarding process that allows you to get reminders about important client dates (anniversary of starting their business, for example)? Can you task your VA with pulling together lists of clients and addresses so that you can send cards and gifts? Can you build time into your calendar to spend reaching out – even if it's just 10 minutes a week?

Do whatever you can to create systems to support you in keeping in touch!

Track your clients first 100 days

When clients come on board, you really want them to stay for the long term. And if that's the case, you must focus on their first 100 days.

The first 100 days can have an impact on your clients' 'stickiness' in your community and will cement their first impression of working with you. Making them feel special and loved is key so they feel like they belong, like they matter to you and that you can really ramp up their own success.

Joey Coleman, in his book, *Never Lose a Customer Again*, talks about the first 100 days and the customer lifecycle, which is about awareness right through to advocacy.[17]

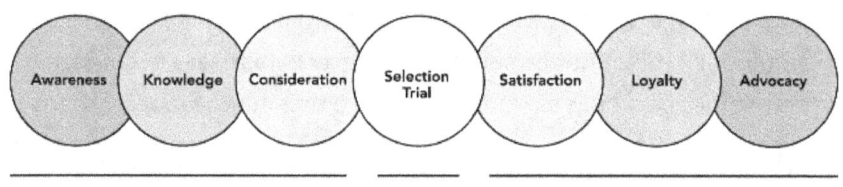

In his book Coleman tells us that across all industries 20% to 70% of newly acquired customers will stop doing business with a company within the first 100 days. His research shows that this is due to a feeling of being neglected in the early stages of their relationship with the business.[18]

Coleman offers a way to dramatically increase customer retention in the first 100 days, setting out eight distinct emotional phases customers go through following a purchase. By understanding these emotions, you can apply techniques – such as in-person meetings, emails, phone calls, mailings, video and even presents – to cement your relationship.[19]

---

[17] Coleman, J. (15 April 2018). Never Lose a Customer Again: Turn Any Sale into Lifelong Loyalty in 100 Days. Portfolio.

[18] Coleman. Never Lose a Customer Again.

[19] Coleman. Never Lose a Customer Again.

Coleman describes the process as being like glue, as it helps the customer to stay connected with you, so you can be focused on supporting them and, in the process, help them to stay with you.[20]

Seth Godin, entrepreneur, best-selling author and speaker, knows a great deal about care. He says, 'Care. Care more than you need to, more often than expected, more completely than the other guy.'

We recently finished a renovation and I was trying to buy some curtains. There were two main curtain companies who were competitors in the market. When looking at the companies, I couldn't really tell which was the better choice – it was neck and neck – so, I decided to just go with the first one.

I called the company, they came out and they showed me three different options. I said I'd have to think about it overnight, but I was pretty keen to get the order sorted as soon as possible because I was sick of the horrible blinds that we had.

The next day I chose the curtains I liked and asked the sales associate to do up a quote for me. She was happy to do that and said, 'I'll send it through by email. And when you get the email it's going to tell you to make a payment and follow a booking process and this and that. But don't do that. Don't follow what it says in the email. Just tell me if you want to go ahead with the order and I'll sort it out.'

So the sales associate did the quote up for me and it was all written in black and white, but the curtains themselves weren't indicated well in the quote. So I wasn't clear on what I was agreeing to purchase.

I messaged her and said, 'I'd like to go ahead but I want to go with the sheer curtains that you showed me, and I can't work out if the ones on the quote are the ones that I liked.' We messaged back and forth and I couldn't seem to work it out so I said, 'Would you mind coming back and

---

[20] Coleman. Never Lose a Customer Again.

showing me again? I'm sorry to muck you around but I really just want to make sure it's right.' So a few days later she came back and went through it all again. And this time when she sent me the quote I told her that I was more than happy to go ahead.

I didn't hear from her for three weeks. Finally I sent her another text and said, 'I want to go ahead with those curtains. I just wanted to see if you got the message. Can we book it in?' When she didn't reply to me again I thought, 'OK. I really wanted to give my business to you but I haven't heard from you. So I'm going to have to go with the other guy.'

I rang the competitors and the sales associate was there the same day, had the right curtains, quoted it all up and was ready to go. I wanted to give it a few days because I wanted to give the other lady a chance since I had asked her to come back a second time. But she didn't respond, didn't acknowledge my message, nothing.

She eventually did come back to me, but I had already had to move on. I said to her, 'I'm really sorry but I've had to go with your competitor because I didn't hear from you. I'm sorry. I would have liked to have done business with you. Hopefully, I can do it again, maybe in future, but I can't help it if I don't hear from you.'

The first 100 days with your customer – whether they have bought from you or just inquired – matter immensely. To build this system into your practice or business you need to take the following steps:

1. First, map the customer journey from the time they first show interest through to engaging you. Understand what happens on the first day, what happens in the first week, what happens in the first month, and what happens in the first year as they're working with you.
2. Second, build in processes that allow you to be engaged, connected and responsive during this time (and ideally beyond!).

When you have these systems in place, you'll be able to keep your customers – and potential customers – engaged with you and your business.

Get to know your 1500s

Kevin Kelly, the founding editor of Wired magazine, once postulated that you only need 1000 true fans to have a sustainable business.[21] The principle is very simple. If you have 1000 true fans who buy everything you create – and you create say $100 a year worth of products or services – then you will earn enough to have a sustainable business.

Seth Godin loved this idea. But expanded it to say that 'you need to alter what you do and how you do it so that 1000 true fans is sufficient to make you very happy.'[22] For me, I think most businesses and practices can easily take on 1500 individuals who are our true fans.

Let's focus on the 1500s. Who are these people? Well your 1500s are people who are following you in your business or want to follow you. These are the people that connect on social media, are customers (or want to be customers) and want to stay in touch. Perhaps they're thinking about working with you in the future, and they want to know more about how you work.

These people may be receiving a newsletter from you, and see your social posts, and they generally care about what you care about. You are solving a problem that they have and they want to be kept in the loop. But because it's such a big number – and they're often a little bit hidden in your business – we sometimes only really pay attention to these people if we're trying to work out why we're not growing.

---

[21] Kelly, K. (4 March 2008). '1,000 True Fans.' The Technium. Available at https://kk.org/thetechnium/1000-true-fans/.

[22] Godin, S. (4 March 2008). '1000 true fans'. Seth's Blog. Available at https://seths.blog/2008/03/1000-true-fans/.

Of course this group is really valuable to keep in mind when you're trying to grow, because they're already primed and ready to work with you.

When it comes to knowing your 1500s, I often think of Monique who was in my community. She was getting a bit behind on sending her newsletter because she didn't really feel like sending it out. She had felt like she was sending it out and getting no traction.

So I said, 'Let's have a look at who's reading your newsletter and paying attention.' And when we dug into the metrics we found an individual that had opened her newsletter 27 times and she had sent it out to other people to read it. It turned out that this person was the head of HR at a global oil and gas company and lived in a neighbouring suburb, but Monique didn't even realise that she'd been so engaged with her practice. She said, 'Oh my God, I'm so embarrassed, I didn't even know this person was on my database.'

This is the problem – we don't know who's on our database. We're not taking the time to look at the reporting each week to see who's paying attention or listening to what we have to say. Because these are the people who have not unsubscribed, they're still there, they're still wanting to hear what you have to say, they still want to know what you believe and they're still looking for your leadership. These are your 1500s.

Kevin Kelly wrote the 1000 True Fans blog in 2008, he likened it to being in a music band.[23] I've got someone in our community, Allison, who loves U2. She will travel across the world to go to a U2 concert. In fact, who's off to Las Vegas to see them at their residency later this year. She's one of U2's 'true fans'.

---

[23] Kelly. 1000 True Fans.

People who are true fans of a music band are the people that will buy every single song that comes out, watch every music video they produce, buy the t-shirts and go to all the concerts. In the same way, your true fans have total buy in for your business. They're listening to what you have to say, watching your posts and videos, reading what you write and buying (or wanting to buy) your services or products. They're there, and so you've got to value them.

Seth Godin says, 'The reason it seems that price is all your customers care about is that you haven't given them something else to care about.' And he's right. What are you doing to get to know them? How are you staying close to them? How are you showing that you care about what they care about and you're listening and paying attention?

So when it comes to caring about your 1500s your first step is to be intentional, strategic and focused on who you are caring about. The second step is to find out what they care about and what is challenging them. This involves being attentive, looking at your data, seeing what things are happening and paying attention to what's going on.

The third step is to give them previews or first looks at things. You can tell them, 'I'm doing this program and I don't want you to miss out. Would you like to have a chat about it before I go to talk to anybody else? It's totally fine if you're not interested, I just didn't want you to miss out.'

The fourth and final step is to get feedback. Find out if you've been really understanding what your 1500s need and if you've been able to help them solve those problems through your thought leadership or services. People like to be involved, and the fact that they've been asked can be quite a powerful thing to create connection and provide real customer care.

Check in on your 150s

Like we discussed above, I agree with Kevin Kelly's 1000 true fans theory. But when it comes to those of us running a practice, then I think that the number of fans (1500 in my theory) is less important than the amount of money per fan or customer. So for those of us running practices or businesses that sell more expensive services or products, I believe that it's the 150 'true fans' or loyal customers or clients that are needed. And because this is a smaller number, you're better able to give more personalised care and nurturing.

The number 150 comes out of the work of social anthropologist Robin Dunbar who posited a layered approach to relationships.[24] His theory was that we have 15 good friends (this is also our 'board of directors' as discussed in the previous chapter), 150 meaningful contacts, 500 acquaintances and 1500 recognisable people (or loyal followers). It's these 150s that form the base of your loyal customers, and a business or practice that lasts[25].

According to Dunbar's work, we only have enough bandwidth to manage meaningful relationships with up to 150 people.[26] And as thought leaders, experts and consultants, this is equally true with our clients.

Matt Church, founder of Thought Leaders, describes your 150s as the people that you would hang out with even if they weren't your clients. These are people that you like, that you share values with and that you genuinely feel a reciprocal loyalty to. That is why they qualify as your 150 meaningful contacts.

When you have a genuine relationship with your clients, you're able to genuinely nurture them. You care about them and their success. So you reach out. You touch base. You follow up. You keep in touch. This is your

---

[24] 'Dunbar's number: Why we can only maintain 150 relationships.' BBC Future. Available at https://www.bbc.com/future/article/20191001-dunbars-number-why-we-can-only-maintain-150-relationships.

[25] Dunbar's number.

[26] Dunbar's number.

culture of care[link to article] – and just like it does with your personal friends, it builds loyalty in those relationships.

Many of us may struggle to find our loyal 150s. It might not feel natural to take business relationships and expand them. You may feel that you're overstepping an invisible boundary. Or you may not even know enough about your clients to know whether or not you like them or have shared values.

This was the case with one of my own clients, Peter. When Peter came to me he had nearly 7500 people on his list. As a productivity expert he was great at what he did, and fantastic at putting in the work and the systems to create this expansive list. But he wanted to grow his business. In fact, he wanted to grow it by 50% that year.

When he came to me the first thing I did was ask him to show me his top 150 customers – those who had bought from him in the past. But even though he'd been in business for 10 years, he wasn't able to show me those top customers.

Once I pushed him he found 40 customers that had bought from him in the past and that he liked. So I asked him what he knew about those 40 people. Why he liked them? But it turned out he didn't know. He didn't really know anything about any of them apart from their roles and the work that he had helped them with. He also wasn't connected in any way – on LinkedIn or Facebook or through any other method. And he hadn't taken any steps to keep in touch or maintain the relationship. He was too transactional.

Building your loyal customer base

When it comes to building your loyal customer base, you can learn from Peter. Spend time and energy on your top 150s. You want to show them that you genuinely care or they're going to feel like just a transaction.

Taking this approach makes economic sense. Research shows that a returning customer will spend 67% more than new customers.[27] And when Peter started to put processes in place around his 150s he found that he was able to genuinely connect with them, and come up with creative (and meaningful) ways to build that mutual loyalty.

He began treating them like friends, rather than transactions, and they responded. At the end of the day he was able to meet his goal of growing his business simply by treating his top customers as friends.

The key – as Peter shows – is to put in place the habits and the routines (the systems!) that allow you to build those relationships. Once you have those in place you'll be in a good position to grow your own 150s.

Ways I have built my 150s

1. Bought a table at a conference and took 10 clients
2. Organised dinners and breakfasts
3. Invited clients to a concert
4. Remembered and celebrated milestones, birthdays and major life events

If you're working to build systems to care for your top 150s you can start by creating a process for identifying and keeping track of those individuals. They start engaging with them. Take some of the steps that I have above – or find some of your own. There are many creative ideas that you can implement to be more inclusive and engaged.

Set up cadences of care

I don't know about you, but I find that sometimes when I'm under a lot of pressure, maybe I'm trying to get my sales going, or trying to deliver,

---

[27] Furgison, L. (2014). '27 Statistics That Prove Repeat Business is Where it's At.' 5 Stars. Available at https://blog.fivestars.com/26-statistics-that-prove-repeat-business-is-where-its-at/.

or I'm travelling and speaking, and trying to juggle everything at once, it can be really hard to still be attention out and care about my customers. That's when having a cadence of care is absolutely critical, and you must have it as part of your systems and your processes so that you don't forget to do it.

One of the things I find when I'm working with experts is that they think that a cadence of care will just. They believe that the people out there that are doing really well in business and caring for their clients are doing that because it's natural to them, they're really good at it or just a caring person. Or they're really good at relationship building, or at staying in touch. But that's not always true. Some people are. But many, many others have spent time learning how to set up cadences of care in their businesses or practices.

The good news is that even if it doesn't feel natural at first, you can get better at care. You don't have to have the caring gene. You just have to have really good systems and processes in place so that you can make sure that you don't forget your customers and clients, and that caring for them is a priority in your practice.

I grew up working for the Mathers family. If you're here in Australia you may have bought your school shoes from a Mathers store. In fact, I worked for Tracy Mathers, the daughter of Sir Robert Mathers, when they were bought out by Kinney Shoes, USA.

I worked for the Mathers family for 12 years. And I learned so much through that experience. But one of the things I really learned from working with them is the value of being a leader in the community and seeing your customers as part of that community.

This was long before social media and YouTube channels, when being a leader in the community meant physically engaging with the community. So, one of the things that I was taught by Tracy – who was an incredible community leader – was to know all our customers by name. Another thing I needed to know was their shoe size off the top of my head.

This made our customers so happy. We kept really good databases and we knew our customers names, shoe size and even the styles of shoes they liked. It was a very personalised service when I worked for Tracy in particular.

This system meant that I had a lot of information about our customers. Because of that I typically sold a lot of the product before it even hit the shelves. In fact, when a shipment came in we would often call our customers and let them know if their favourite brand was in and that we had them in their size nine. We'd offer to pop them aside but ensure that we weren't pressuring them or being salesy. We'd say, 'If not, that's totally fine. I just didn't want you to miss out.'

This level of care was one of the reasons that the stores were so successful and why we were able to get the revenue up and grow the businesses and the stores like we did.

When we're in a community and when we are leading a community, our job is to keep an eye out for those people who are perhaps struggling or who maybe don't ask for help. There will always be a squeaky wheel – and some will be like that. But there's others that you really need to keep an eye on.

Marketing and social media guru Gary Vee said that the best marketing strategy ever is care. I love that the guru of marketing is so focused on care. And I love that it's about intent as opposed to content. Most experts and business owners will create a lot of content, but it's far more about the intention than it is about just spraying people with content and hustle.

I like to think of it like having money in the bank. If you are focussed on the cadence of care, then it's a bit like putting money into the account and saving it for another day. It's not about ringing people and saying, 'Hey, buy my thing!' It's more about generously noticing and connecting in an authentic way.

So you might see someone on a panel and send them a text, saying. 'Hey, you did an awesome job on the panel.' If you see them on TV you might say, 'I noticed you're on Sky Business today. You did an awesome job. Just wanted to say how good it was.' People will love that you took the time to notice them. You paid attention and they really get a lot of value from that. They're thrilled that you noticed and that you actually have some words of encouragement for them and to keep them going.

The systems you need to get into this cadence of care are two fold. The first is focused around curiosity. It means paying attention, reaching out, asking 'how are you going? What's happening in your world? How did Sky Business go last week? You did an awesome job, but how was it? The second is around being generous in your communications and with sharing things proactively. Maybe each quarter you find a book, or maybe you find an article for someone or maybe you just send them a personal card, whatever it might be. Instead of sitting back and waiting for them to come to you, you get a rhythm and a sense of activity and momentum going with the intention of engaging and connecting.

So how do you do this? How do you set up a system of care around your 150s?

First of all, you need to tag your 150s. Make sure that you know exactly who those people are or who they will be. Even if you only have three people that are going to be part of that 150 group – identify them. The

Secondly, I recommend that every Mondayyou have a database meeting where you go through those 150s. In my practice, it's the first meeting of the week, because we know that if we don't have those 150s, we don't have a practice. We talk about what we noticed that week, and look at what's happening for our clients. Sue got a new dog. But we haven't seen photos of the new dog yet, so we go and check out the puppy on Facebook. And then we reach out and say congrats on the cute new puppy! This comes out of the database meeting, and it just makes me stay focused on the right people and not lose focus on the wrong people.

The third thing you could do to have a cadence of care is to have a creative sales meeting. These meetings are about paying attention to what's going on in the world. Imagine you do a lot of work in the leadership space in financial services. So maybe you've been reading about something a particular bank is going through. From here you think about what this could mean for your practice? What's going on in the world? How does this impact the people in your community? And who can we proactively reach out to?

Customer acquisition and retention

When you're running a busy growing practice, the people you have around you really matter. And like every business owner, you're going to have fantastic clients who may choose to move on.

The problem is that when those we love working with someone and they choose to move on from us it can feed our own fears. The biggest of these is the fear that our practice or business will fail because we don't have any clients.

The truth is that churn – both client churn and employee churn – can certainly have a negative impact on any business. 40-60% of customers leave after using a product or service just one time.[28] And the cost of acquiring a new customer vastly outweighs the costs of keeping your current clients.[29]

---

[28] Walker, T. (23 December 2022). 'A Quick Guide to Successful User Onboarding for SaaS Products'. CXL. Available at https://cxl.com/blog/quick-guide-user-onboarding-saas-products/.

[29] Landis, T. (12 April 2022). 'Customer Retention Marketing vs. Customer Acquisition Marketing.' Outbound Engine. Available at https://www.outboundengine.com/blog/customer-retention-marketing-vs-

The answer to this churn is to increase our retention of employees. But how?

How to increase retention rate

After a recent renovation I needed to reset my studio up. This meant some new tech to help me manage the various elements that I use in my own practice. I did some research, and thought I had settled on getting a new iMac. So I headed to our local JB HiFi.

The store was quite busy, so when I spoke to the gentleman behind the counter I simply told him what I was looking for, without getting into all the details of my practice and needs. But instead of just giving me what I wanted, he stopped to ask me what I needed it for.

I explained everything. He patiently listened and then said, 'I think you just need this console rather than a whole new computer'. He showed me what I needed, and the total cost was less than $300. And while they didn't have it in stock, he said, 'I'll write it all down and I can order it in for you. And I'll ensure you get it all set up. Just take a photo of your office set up and give me a call.'

I did what he said and the result was that I ended up with an excellent solution that was far more affordable for my particular needs. He didn't try to sell me a more expensive product that I didn't really need. Instead, he tried to solve my problem for me. And this was all because he cared enough to give me his time, energy and, most importantly, care.

So, when it comes down to how to increase your retention rates, it all comes down to care. The number one thing that will make a difference in your retention rates of both clients and staff – and drive your retention rate increase tenfold – is your level of care.

---

customer-acquisition-marketing/#:~:text=Acquiring%20a%20new%20customer%20can,customer%20is%205%2D20%25..

Of course you need robust systems in place to support this level of care. If you don't have the right systems in place, you will burn both yourself and your staff out as you try to be everything to everybody.

Having care doesn't mean giving so much that it impacts your own success. And the right systems help you show care without burning out. This might be a Christmas card list in your CRM. Or a list of birthdays. Or it could be a regular review of client's socials allowing you to celebrate their wins or get in touch when other life events come up. Even just a rotating schedule that allows you to consistently 'check in' with clients can make a huge difference in your practice. As long as it works for you, that's what matters.

When you get the systems right, you'll be in a position to increase your retention rate by up to 10x your current level. This will have a direct impact on your conversions, cash flow and ultimate success. And you'll also have happier clients and staff (both good things).

Retention Rate Model

	Activity	Growth	Retention
5	Care	Growth	10X
4	Prioritisation	Belonging	5X
3	Attention	Time	2X
2	Mindfulness	Community	0
1	Careless	Awareness	-1X

To get started take a look at where you fall in the actions and focus areas currently. Are you mindful and building a community? That's great. But your next step is to move from mindful to paying attention and from community to personal time?

As you move along the actions in the model, your focus changes, taking you from unaware (and with too much churn!) all the way through to the growth of your clients and team (with 10x the retention rate).

To move along this model ask yourself:

1. Where are you on the Retention Rate Model?
2. What steps can you take to implement the next level up?
3. What systems do you need to implement to help you level up?

Conclusion

Developing the mindset of customer care, devoting your time and energy to it generously and putting into practice systems to support that, will move you along the spectrum of customer care from overtly salesy to truly nurturing. And that will bring you incredible results.

Now, you just need to do the same for your team!

CHAPTER 6

TEAM CARE

Mindset

Caring for our team should be one of the easiest nurturing we do. After all, we know our team. They're close by. We speak to them often. We can easily hear about their day, their problems, their challenges and their wins. But unfortunately, we just don't always take the time to do that.

Why not? We're busy. We're distracted. We're thinking about our customers and clients. And sometimes we just haven't built in the mindset, the generosity that gives us the space and time to nurture and the systems to support us in doing that.

But we can. Here's how.

Team member for life

If you've travelled to Shibuya, Japan, you may be familiar with the story of Hachiko, the faithful and loyal Akita dog.[1] For years, Hachiko accompanied his master Professor Elizaburo Ueno each day to Shibuya

---

[1] Koh, I. (23 June 2019). 'Hachiko Statue in Shibuya. Japan's most popular meeting point in the heart of Tokyo'. Japan Travel. Available at https://en.japantravel.com/tokyo/hachiko-statue-in-shibuya/44644.

Station. On Professor Ueno's return from Tokyo's Imperial University each afternoon, Hachiko would be waiting to greet him.

One afternoon, Professor Ueno did not return, as he had died while at work. For the next 10 years, Hachiko continued to walk to Shibuya Station, every day, to wait for Professor Ueno, until his own death.

Mark and I recently travelled to Tokyo and were able to see the statue of Hachiko at the Shibuya Station.

While thinking of his story, I was reminded of the value of loyalty in a broader sense – as well as within our own practices and businesses. I believe that loyalty is becoming increasingly important, particularly within your team. But rather than bemoaning the fact that people are becoming less loyal (an arguable contention regardless), we should be looking at ways to build our team loyalty and grow an exceptional team?

To understand how to build team loyalty we first need to understand why it matters. Quiet quitting gives us some insight.

Quiet quitting

According to McCrindle research, the average tenure in a job in Australia is three years four months.[2] But there are many other employees that aren't actually leaving their roles, but are simply 'quiet quitting'.

In fact, quiet quitting has become a global phenomenon. It's where 'unmotivated, disinterested, checked-out employees' determine that rather than leaving a role where they're unhappy or feel undervalued, they'll simply do the bare minimum or even underperform at work.[3]

As a leader in your practice, managing this kind of disengagement in your team while trying to focus on growth seems like an impossible task. But engaging, inspiring and motivating your team to build loyalty to you long-term, while also helping them to achieve their potential, is possible. The answer lies in your employees' happiness at work.

I'm accredited in The Science of Happiness at Work program, which teaches why happiness at work is important and how to go about

---

[2] 'Job mobility in Australia'. McCrindle. Available at https://mccrindle.com.au/article/job-mobility-in-australia/.

[3] Herway, J. (24 October 2022). 'Need an Answer to Quiet Quitting? Start With Your Culture.' Gallup. Available at https://www.gallup.com/workplace/403598/need-answer-quiet-quitting-start-culture.aspx.

increasing it.[4] I believe deeply in this research because when your team is happy at work, they are engaged and productive.

Jessica Pryce-Jones' four years of research into what happiness means in a work context – and why it matters in human and financial terms – led to her book, *Happiness at Work: Maximizing Your Psychological Capital for Success*. Jessica found that happiness at work is a mindset. It enables leaders, consultants, and employees alike to act to maximise their performance and achieve their potential. In a nutshell then, what makes employees happy at work is achieving their potential.[5]

Are your team members achieving their potential?

This leads to the question – are your team members achieving their potential? What's important to me as a team leader, is to provide stability, job security, training and opportunities for my staff. This helps them to achieve their goals both at work and in other areas of their life.

When I am recruiting, I like to employ the 'high performance model'. This is a model developed by Matt Church and Peter Cook of Thought Leaders.

---

[4] Neff, K. 'The Science of Happiness at Work.' Greater Good Science Centre. Available at https://ggsc.berkeley.edu/what_we_do/online_courses_tools/the_science_of_happiness_at_work.

[5] Pryce-Jones, J. (2011). Happiness at Work: Maximizing Your Psychological Capital for Success. Wiley.

As you can see, there are two halves to the model:

The top half is what I need in my practice from my team to 'make my life easier'. This 'service' includes honesty, working each day to achieve your potential and commitment.

The bottom half is what I provide for my team when they are working, 'to make their life better'. This 'fulfilment' includes support, stability, job security, training, opportunities to master their work, and acknowledging the unique attributes that they bring to the team.

Both halves are centred around the mindset of team care. It's this mindset that guides the care that I show my team and we show each other. This is evident in our support of each other. In fact, one of my team, MC, needed job security and a good income to get married and buy a home. So I worked with MC to set personal milestones so he could achieve his goals. But of course we were able to do so because we had a mindset of care.

Creating a growth opportunity mindset

Part of your team care mindset is to look for growth opportunities, and this is another way to build team loyalty. Be honest too. If you realise a person is no longer a good fit for your team. The thing that could 'make their life better' is helping them to move on to a new role. This is where it's about more than the individual and realising their own potential – it's about the impact on you and your whole team.

Recognising growth opportunities for your team can be part of your annual performance reviews, quarterly check ins and even daily huddles.

Steps

If you're keen to understand how to build team loyalty through happiness at work and embracing a mindset of team care, here are some steps to take:

1. Understand the vision your team members each have for themselves.
2. Help them to break down their goals for work and life outside work.
3. Be interested in your team. Who are they outside of work? How was their weekend? What do they have going on that could impact their work life?
4. Check in. Know what works for each person – daily, weekly, monthly, annually. Create certainty for them by letting them know they are valued and important to your practice.
5. Create a culture. Build the idea of team care into your team culture. This will ensure that you're looking after each other well.

Seek first to understand then to be understood

When you're working with your team, you need to always make generous assumptions. People do things that might sometimes seem a bit strange to you. They may even make decisions that feel stupid or ridiculous. And you might ask yourself how they could possibly think it was a good idea.

But people don't do things just to be stupid or silly or even just to annoy you. People, more often than not, are doing things for reasons that seem perfectly sensible to themselves. They'll take actions based on their experiences and their own understanding about the world. And more often than not, they're doing the best they can.

So if you can create generous assumptions, rather than being angry or upset, you'll be able to embrace curiosity and find out why they took the action they did. This helps you to show respect – respect for their thinking and even the actions they took. Your team members won't be made to feel stupid, and will instead feel supported and listened to. And it will help you to learn. We don't want to shut people down because what I've learned is that sometimes their reasoning is even better than our own. But we can't know that if we don't seek first to understand.

When you give generous assumptions and adopt a curiosity mindset you are opening the door first rather than just trying to shut it down. And this door can often become a gateway to innovation. You might find a way to do something better and identify gaps that you never saw before.

Stephen Covey, in his book *The 7 Habits of Highly Effective People*, talks about seeking to understand first and then to be understood.[6] Listen, then make your point, then discuss the best way forward in order to stop this happening again or to get a better outcome next time.

I often think about the story of a woman who stopped at the traffic lights and then failed to go when the lights turned green. The gentleman sitting behind her started beeping the horn and shouting, 'Come on, hurry up. The light's going to go red.' Once it did turn back to red he got out of the car to give her an earful only to find her leaning over the back trying to stop her child from choking.

We just don't know people's reasons. It's up to you as a leader to be curious enough to find out what those reasons are that your team is making decisions, and what to change in the future so we're on the same page.

As Einstein said, 'Peace cannot be kept by force, it can only be achieved by understanding.' And if you can take the time to understand why someone has done something a certain way, you'll have better insight and it'll also help you to look out for potential potholes in future.

To have generous assumptions with your team, start by listening and then asking, 'Can you tell me a bit about what happened here? What made you think about going that way?'

Once you've listened to understand the response, you can then consider the reasons, and make your suggestions if needed. Don't come in over

---

[6] Covey, S. (9 November 2004). The 7 Habits of Highly Effective People: Powerful Lessons in Personal Change. Free Press.

the top of them. Don't trample on them. Just be mindful that most people are trying to do their best and be respectful when you make suggestions. Talk to them the way you'd like someone to speak to you.

Love languages

Love languages might not be the first thing you think about when it comes to your team. But having a love mindset is vitally important. Because when you understand the love language or appreciation language of your team, you can start to show how you care in a meaningful way.

How do love languages work? Well there are particular love languages, but in general, it's about being mindful about what each team member will resonate with and then ensuring that any connection you make with them is based upon those things that will be meaningful. It's a little bit like being in another country where you speak the same language but where there is a different culture. You need to find the right way to relate to each other in this new country – and if you don't apply yourself, this can easily be lost in translation.

Dr Gary Chapman wrote the *New York Times* bestselling book, *5 Love Languages*. In it he talks about the five types of love languages to show you appreciate people. These are:

1. **Words of affirmation.** This includes compliments and those types of things.
2. **Physical touch.** This is connection in a physical way.
3. **Gifts.** This involves buying people presents and gifts.
4. **Acts of service.** This is doing things for people.
5. **Time.** This involves giving people the time and attention that they need.[7]

---

[7] Chapman, G. (2015). Five Love Languages Revised Edition: The Secret to Love That Lasts. Strand Publishing.

I worked for a boss many years ago, who was fabulous, and her love language was gifts. At that time, I was fresh out of uni and I didn't have any money. My boss bought really high-end luxury goods for me, which was lovely, but gifts are not my love language. And because of that they don't necessarily motivate me as much as they might others. Instead, I'm a words of affirmation person. I love cards and the written word. A card, email or text saying, 'Thank you so much. I really appreciate all your help.'

It wasn't that I didn't appreciate the beautiful gifts, but she didn't necessarily need to go to the expense that she did. If she had known my love language, she probably could have saved herself a lot of money.

It was Gandhi who said, 'Relationships are based on four principles. Respect, understanding, acceptance, and appreciation.' As a nurturing leader being able to identify what love language your team speaks means you can tap into that and allow you to show your appreciation in a way that is meaningful to them.

Being encouraging

When it comes to your team, it's important that you are always focused on encouraging your team. People are hard enough on themselves. You don't need to add to that. People struggle to see the positives in themselves most days, and, as we know, languish under negative self-talk. They can feel like they try so hard, and just don't get any traction, dealing with constant interruptions and distractions. Because of this they can feel overwhelmed. And then they have to go home and come back tomorrow and do it all again.

The more that you can help your team to find hope, lightness and possibility, and bring ideas of a positive way forward in their work each day, the more they can feel like there's a light at the end of the tunnel. They'll feel a relief that it's not always going to be Groundhog Day.

Tom Rath said, 'If you want people to understand that you value their contributions and that they are important, the recognition and praise you provide must have meaning that is specific to each individual.' So when you are encouraging your team, you need to be aware of them specifically – that way you can provide specific encouragement. A team member will respond better to a comment like, 'You did a great job with that report. I especially appreciated the time you spent on the analysis', then they will to feedback like, 'Great job.'

To be able to offer specific encouragement, go outside yourself. Notice what's going on. Pay attention to what your team members are doing, and if they do something really great, tell them. And if they're feeling a bit flat or downtrodden, check in how they're going and find a way to encourage them. Really step into that empathy so you can show them that you get how they feel.

You could also consider sending them a motivational card. I send cards in the post to my team and to my clients if I feel like they're going through a bit of a tough time. My goal is to help keep them going, keep the tires pumped up and show them that I really care.

Create a culture of feedback

Encouragement can often come in the form of feedback, but some leaders and teams think of feedback as a negative event. But that's because those leaders only give feedback when there is a problem. On the other hand, if you;re always giving positive feedback only, you can come across as insincere.

But when your feedback is balanced and includes constructive and encouraging words, and given with respect and sensitivity, this creates a sense that you are a leader that cares. Because of this your team will treat your comments with credibility and respect, they'll embrace the growth and opportunities you present. This type of feedback makes it safe to fail because your team recognises that you will give them a chance to try again, and that means you will cultivate high performance and growth. As Mother Theresa said, 'Failure is merely feedback that there is something blocking the path of the emergence and expansion of the greatest version of yourself'.

Sue Anderson, an expert in feedback fitness, has undertaken research on the types of feedback that women and men appear to find easier to give. What she found is that both women and men felt the most confident giving 'acknowledgement feedback' – this is commentary on what you are doing well – with women feeling slightly more confident than men. On the other hand, men felt more confident with providing 'evaluation feedback' – which evaluates how an individual is performing or going – and with 'guidance feedback' – which is how an individual can do better.[8]

Interestingly, women felt more 'clumsy' when giving feedback generally (19.7% women versus 4.7% of men), but more courageous at the same time. But perhaps we can push through those feelings of unease and uncertainty by taking the balanced approach to feedback, because it's through this balanced approach that you, as a leader, can get the most out of your team.

So, when you're providing feedback, always be mindful of answering the question, 'Am I keeping things balanced here?' Because anyone can fall into doing this wrong. But if you do, it can leave you and your team feeling like you're never winning. But if you can keep it balanced you'll find that your team will be more motivated, more inspired and more dedicated to improving all the time.

---

[8] Anderson, S. 'Is your feedback equal?' Sue Anderson Blog. Available at https://www.sue-anderson.com.au/blog/is-your-feedback-equal.

Be your number one customer

When growing a business, we often default to prioritising customers, which is great. But when we focus too much on our customers, and not enough on our team, it can really affect our ability to grow together. So what we need to do is ensure that 'you' – and that's your entire team – is your number one customer.

When you treat your team as your number one customer you'll prioritise them. And when you prioritise your team they'll know that you value them, and you'll find that you have more clarity, more space and more energy to grow your business together.

Without that prioritisation, your team might feel like your only focus is on the customer, while they're just a cog in the wheel. They might feel that they don't matter, and that everything you do revolves solely around the customer. Of course, things do generally revolve around customers in any business, but the fact of the matter is that you can't help anyone – especially your customers – if your team isn't functional.

It was Paulo Coehlo, the famous Brazilian novelist, who said, 'When you say yes to others, make sure you are not saying no to yourself.' And this is so true when it comes to caring for your team. You have to really make sure that you're always keeping that balance.

In my own team, we were facing a challenge to get our team meetings done on Mondays when we had them scheduled. But I had a lot of client meetings on Mondays and I was often trying to get on top of everything for the week ahead. It all became just too much. But we still wanted to prioritise our team. So we decided to leave Monday mornings for getting on top of everything and Monday afternoon for seeing clients, and we started scheduling Tuesdays as our team day. We don't book any clients on Tuesdays anymore. It's our time to get ourselves organised and make sure we've got what we need as a team and without trying to compete with all the other priorities.

A study by BetterUp, found people need to have relationships with five friendly colleagues at work to feel connected.[9] Connection is vital because it impacts how our teams feel, perform and grow at work. Those who feel connected have more wellbeing and the workplaces benefited too, having more customer engagement and boosted profit.[10]

So what can you do to make your team your number one customer? As yourself:

1. When are you prioritising your team over customers or customers over your team? How are you getting that balance right? Or how are you getting it wrong?
2. How can you build connection with your team?
3. How can you advocate for your team more?

Generosity

Understanding the importance of your team helps you to put in place the elements you need to have a team care mindset. But in order to make it effective you have to be generous with yourself and your team as well.

Expressions & mood

Research shows that employees who woke up on the wrong side of the bed are 10% less productive each day.[11] But intervening to reset their

---

[9] Eatough, E. (20 September 2022). 'Why workplace friendships are key to managing negative emotions on the job.' BetterUp. Available at https://www.betterup.com/blog/connections-improve-mental-health.

[10] Eatough. Why workplace friendships are key.

[11] Rothbard, N. (May 2011). 'Mood and Productivity: Undoing a Bad Start.' Wharton Aresty Institute of Executive Education; University of Pennsylvania. Available at https://executiveeducation.wharton.upenn.edu/thought-leadership/wharton-

mood also reset their productivity. And that's great news! However, in order to help to reset your teams' moods you need to be able to read them – and that comes down to reading expressions and body language.

When you're able to read your team, you can navigate the complexity of emotions that are really going on under the surface. You might have people who are struggling with challenges at work or at home, who are being fake or inauthentic or who are afraid to speak up. There could be even cultural differences, and sometimes even things like the fear of losing their job if they really say what they think.

So to read your team you need to get really good at identifying if someone's being congruent, truthful and authentic, or if they're not saying what they would really like to say. If you can read facial expressions, it's a little bit like having access to a truth serum. When you can do that you can get to the heart of a problem, and then you're in a position to really try to resolve it in a respectful way.

Paul Ekman wrote the really great book *Emotions Revealed* about emotional intelligence. In it he talks about the roots of our emotions and how these emotions are revealed on the face giving clear signals about what is really going on to anyone who is focused on reading them.[12]

Dr Daniel Goleman, psychologist and leading researcher on empathy that we mentioned in the last chapter, says that people's emotions are rarely put into words; far more often they are expressed through other cues. So the key to intuiting others' feelings is in the ability to read tone of voice, gestures and facial expressions.

---

at-work/2011/05/productivity-and-mood/#:~:text=A%20recent%20study%20indicates%20that,falls%20by%20over%2010%20percent.

[12] Ekman, P. (2007). *Emotions Revealed, Second Edition: Recognizing Faces and Feelings to Improve Communication and Emotional Life*. Holt Paperbacks. Available at https://www.amazon.com.au/Emotions-Revealed-Paul-Ekman/dp/0805083391.

When I first started working as a manager at the Mathers stores I was extremely focused on just getting sales in and the store productive. But my boss, Tracy, would sometimes say something like, 'Did you notice that Lorraine didn't really seem herself today?' And I'd go, 'Oh, really? Didn't she?' And she'd say, 'Yeah, you need to get onto that.'

Reading your team's facial expressions and body language does take time and focus – and that's where generosity comes in. You have to be generous with your time and energy so you can focus on this important work.

I had a really great coach to help me build my leadership skills, and, over time, body language and facial expressions. And this served me well because when I was in my 20s, I was working with people who were in their 40s, 50s, 60s and 70s, and they were not very impressed with having a young manager. There were a lot of glances with each other and conversations held in hushed undertones, and I had to be able to try and read all that.

I was really good at being able to get sales and a high-performing store, but now I needed to learn how to read and connect with people who were often quite a lot older than me. So I ended up enrolling in a lie detector course, so I could learn how to identify if people were telling me the truth or not. I had always taken people at their word previously so I didn't necessarily understand the expressions that were in their faces. But the course taught me that a big part of reading people's expressions and body language is listening to your instincts. So I started to trust myself, and when I would notice something that would look off, I would simply ask the other person. I learned how to pick up on people's emotions and figure out what was really going on underneath.

When you're in this situation, how are you picking up people's emotions? Can you tell if they're having a bad day? Can you tell if they're having a good day? What does normal look like? What does stress look like? Can you tell the difference?

Most importantly, would you know how to do that with any of your team? What would you do? What would you say to them? Some good choices might be, 'I just noticed that you seem a little bit off today. Are you OK?' Or, 'You seem a little bit tired,' or, 'You seem a little bit stressed about this. Are you all right?'

Reading those facial expressions and body language can help you get to the heart of any problem with your team – even when they're hesitant (or afraid) to speak up. And then you'll be in a position to really try to resolve it in a respectful way.

Surprise & delight

Another way that you can be generous with your team is by focusing on how to surprise and delight them. I'm not always great with surprises. My husband, Mark, is so good at it. But I'm organised and structured and planned – none of which aligns very well with spontaneity and surprises. But I understand how well it can work in a team environment.

In fact, Mark is really good at relationship building and he knows the value of surprising and delighting. He's always organising events, trips and dinners. We went to Cirque du Soleil the other day. He blocks time in my calendar and says surprise. And it's so fun and it brings lightness and joy into my otherwise very planned life.

It's the same with your team. Most of the time their work is going to be very planned, and will simply follow their regular day-to-day routine. Experiencing something that's unexpected and above and beyond is not the norm. But when you do it, people love it. It makes them feel valued and a priority. And it makes them feel cared about and nurtured. You're doing something that's not expected and that didn't have to be done – they could go on with their daily work just fine without it. But you did do it and that's exceptional.

how much delivered

bored	delight
ignore	anger

how easy or important

When it comes to surprising and delighting, there are two variables. The first is how much did you deliver and the second is how easy or important was it? In one of these quadrants is delight, which is where you really surprise your team and they really value it. If you can't do this your team might get bored and lose inspiration and motivation.

In the other quadrant it shows where you might have delivered something but it didn't really delight your team. In that case, they'll either ignore you or they'll actually be angry with you, because what you did had no impact. This is like gifting someone with a pencil at Christmas.

I love Seth Godin's quote where he says, 'Surprise and delight and connection are remarkable.' He's right. I remember receiving an amazing gift from Gihan Perera who I referred for a conference and keynote. He sent me a beautiful hamper with flowers and goodies and all sorts of lovely things. It was just beautiful. Because it was totally unexpected it made me feel really good. In his way, he's built me into his team now.

So if you need to implement surprise and delight in your business to nurture your team what are some of the things you can do? Number one is our personalised events. Find things that you can do that your team really enjoys. Another thing you can do are random acts of kindness. Just simple things like picking up lunch for them when you're going out. Or bringing coffee for the whole team. The third thing to do is to make it part of your DNA.

So whilst it's a surprise and delight for others, it needs to be very intentional and systemised for you and your practice or business. This will help you to see opportunities, notice things and surprise people.

Shine the light on others

The great Confucius once said, 'Don't worry about being acknowledged by others; worry about failing to acknowledge them.'

When people step into a leadership role, they can often think that means they'll also take centre stage. But in fact, you need to be generous in your positioning and actually take a backseat. This is known as humble leadership.

Humble leadership is really about you stepping out of the spotlight and finding ways to make others shine. This means appreciating them and helping them to stand out. Humble leadership embraces the idea that leadership is ultimately about service, not status. And when it comes to your team, it's a fantastic way to increase retention. In fact, 53% of employees say they would stay longer at their company if they felt more appreciation from their leader.[13]

I like to think of it as being the man behind the curtain like. Rather than being centre stage, you're now off in the wings, helping to make sure that those on stage are able to deliver a flawless performance. You're not the one on stage. You're not saying, 'Look at me!' Now you're really focused on what you need to do to support your team and help them to be their best.

---

[13] (13 November 2013). 'Employers To Retain Half Of Their Employees Longer If Bosses Showed More Appreciation; Glassdoor Survey.' Glassdoor for Employers. Available at https://www.glassdoor.com/employers/blog/employers-to-retain-half-of-their-employees-longer-if-bosses-showed-more-appreciation-glassdoor-survey/.

How do you do this? Be generous with your time and energy and help them to remove roadblocks and find ways to progress so they can feel like they're achieving their potential. I believe in this so wholeheartedly I even have my own podcast, called *Shining the Light*. And on this I just interview incredible people. I spend almost no time talking about myself or what I'm doing. It's about shining the light on other people.

As a result, meeting planners and conference organisers that follow me then engage these incredible people to speak at their conferences and events. And it feels great to help connect them.

As you step more into leadership, you'll have more opportunities to facilitate bringing people together, connecting them and helping them to achieve their potential. Taking these opportunities to shine the light on others will really take you from a leader, to an exceptional leader.

When it comes to determining whether you're shining the light on others, ask yourself:

1. What can you share about others' success at work?
2. Is there someone who's done something really well this week?
3. Can you share this on your socials, in a podcast or even send a message around to everybody.
4. Think about all the different ways that you can acknowledge people. Even ask them if you're not sure what they might like. You can do a survey and ask them how they like to be acknowledged.

You're not a mind reader, and you're not expected to be a mind reader. But you're expected to try and work out a way to help them feel like they're recognised so that they're feeling fulfilled, winning and achieving their potential.

Say thank you

It doesn't take a lot to express gratitude and say thank you. But when we want people to grow and achieve their potential, we need to nurture them in a way that motivates them to repeat the positive behaviours that allow that growth. And gratitude does just that.

When we say thank you for something that your team has done they're more likely to repeat that behaviour and make the same choices again. It also increases your own vibration, how you resonate and connect with people because you become one of those leaders that people want to be around, who express gratitude and optimism rather than focusing on the negative. And at the end of the day, gratitude helps everyone grow – you as a leader, the team and the organisation as a whole.

My very first boss was a woman called June Ma, whom I just adored. I started working for her when I was 14, and she was so sweet and lovely and perhaps a little bit naive. But she was incredibly caring, and she really cultivated and cared about her staff.

I remember whenever I would work for her during school holidays we would put in really big days. And every single day after we would pack up the shop and pull down the shutter, she would say, 'Thanks so much for your day!'

It was a little thing, but it meant a lot because as I went along in my life and my career I found that I didn't always hear it very much. And I'm not the only one who has had that experience. But it's a shame, because gratitude is something that is really valuable and important to say to your own team each day, if you can.

Eckhart Tolle who said, 'Acknowledging the good that you already have in your life is the foundation for all abundance.' The more you can be generous in your gratitude, saying thank you often and not feeling frustrated, you'll cross the gap between what you want to have done by your team and how you want them to be working together and where they are.

Gratitude can actually help you and your team to achieve more. Research set out in *Leading with Gratitude*, shows that gratitude to employees is the fastest and least costly way to boost your team performance.[14]

When I think about this work, I return to the research of Jessica Pryce-Jones on happiness at work. In her research, she found five key areas that help people to feel like they're achieving their potential and ultimately lead them to feel engaged and happy in their work.

The first area she speaks about is important in the context of gratitude, and that is the notion of contribution. When people feel they are contributing they also feel like they're making a difference. So as a nurturing leader, we've got to help our team to see that line of sight between what they do every single day and how they contribute to the ultimate vision and goal. To really achieve potential, it all comes back to purpose. And gratitude helps them see that line of sight.

In my own practice I tend to be working with clients all the time, but I'm also really mindful that we have a wider team. So if one of our clients has a real win or some kind of success, I recognise that while I might be the coach, there's five other people on my team who have helped that success happen. So the win is shared with the entire team, I thank them for their help and we celebrate together. I make sure that they know that I couldn't do my work if it wasn't for them. It's important to keep that sense of contribution and that line of sight there.

So my question to you is, how often are you thanking your team? Ideally, you're doing so each day or – at least – each week. And are you specific in your thanks? Expressing gratitude for a specific task done well aligns the team for doing more of that into the future, which is great for your team overall. And when you thank people for something that they did, it goes a long way to helping people feel like they're valued, that they have

---

[14] Gostick, A & Elton, C. (2020). Leading with Gratitude: Eight Leadership Practices for Extraordinary Business Results. Harper Business.

something to contribute, and helps them to become more engaged and high-performing.

Systems

As with both self-care and customer care, the final element of team care is to create systems that support your ability to really nurture your team. In this way you can take the mindset and generosity and make practical changes that you can put to work each day.

And you should start by asking your team how they are… really.

Asking how your team are… really

One of the best ways to implement care for your team is to make it a habit to ask how they are. And not a habit that becomes mindless. One that really allows you to find out what is going on in their lives. And to do that you need to get specific.

You're not trying to pry, and unless you're very close, you don't want to go too deep into the really personal things. It's just being a bit curious and interested. As Dale Carnegie, American lecturer, author and pioneer in the field of public speaking and the psychology of the successful personality, says, 'You can make more friends in two months by becoming interested in other people than you can in two years by trying to get other people interested in you.'

So simply ask about things that are happening in their lives – from how their sports game was on the weekend to where they went on their holiday. You might ask how was their son's birthday party? Or did they enjoy the book they mentioned? Being interested means you'll have a deeper connection with your team and they'll feel more valued and have a sense that you really do care about them.

We've already talked about connection in the workplace, but it bears repeating again. Research shows that disconnected employees cost US companies up to $406 billion a year through higher turnover, lower productivity, more absenteeism and lower quality of work. On the other hand, those companies that put a priority on employee connection found a reduction in each of those negative factors and increased profit overall.[15]

Tracy Mathers and her father, Sir Robert Mathers, were the best at reaching out to find out how their staff was. Because of that they really understood what was happening for their team and what was going on in their world. And this meant that they were able to be a little more proactive, and it taught me, in the 12 years that I worked with them, to be interested in my team.

Tracy would come to me to talk about the team and she'd say to me, 'What's happening with Lorna's husband? Ted's not very well at the moment. Have you found out about that?' And I'd say, 'Oh, I don't know. I haven't asked. I don't want to pry.' And she'd say, 'It's not prying. You're just caring. If she doesn't want to tell you, she won't tell you. But I think you need to find these things out because it means that we can make sure she's OK, but we can also run the business at the same time.'

It's important to try to be like the Mathers, and find out how your staff is. You don't have to know every tiny detail about them, but definitely understand the big things. Do they have children? What do they do on weekends? What do they like doing outside of work? Do they play sport?

---

[15] Poswolsky, A. (21 January 2022). 'How Leaders Can Build Connection in a Disconnected Workplace.' *Harvard Business Review*. Available at https://hbr.org/2022/01/how-leaders-can-build-connection-in-a-disconnected-workplace.

If you're not very good at this stuff, you're not alone. But that's where systems come in. One simple way to keep track of your staff is to write it down.

I'm not very good at remembering things, so I keep a notebook. This means I've got it all written down. This is vital for my clients but not as important for my team which is quite small and who I know very well. But if you have a large team then you must write it down. That way when you're meeting with a member of your team you have notes to remind yourself of what is going on with them. This also frees up your mental space so you don't have to rely so much on trying to remember.

Coach every day

Checking in and asking your team how they are is important. But it's also vital that you're providing them with opportunities to grow and develop. So it's not enough to just check in on your team and say hi. It's really about checking in on their goals for the day, what is standing in their way, what they need from you. And you do this by coaching every day.

Coaching helps your team to move from feeling stuck through to feeling like they're succeeding. And when you can do this they'll really start to have a sense of feeling valued and committed to their work each day.

As a coach it would seem that it's easy for me to coach my own team. But in fact, I need systems to remind me to coach every day just as much as the next person. Years ago I had two team members who were moved into another area of the organisation that I was working in at the time. I was on one side of the team and they were way over the other, and in some ways it felt like they were the naughty children who had been kicked out. They weren't particularly happy about it, and I wasn't very happy about it because I didn't have them nearby. Nevertheless, we tried to be adaptable and go with it.

Over time I realised that they were actually feeling a bit neglected. I could feel rumblings and I thought, 'OK, I need to come by.' I spoke to my boss about it and her advice was that I needed to, 'coach every day.' She said, 'Check in with them each day, and you'll be able to help them feel like they're not ostracised and that they're being included.' Once I started doing that, the problems went away and we had a really tight team.

Coaching leads to behavioural changes in your team. And the research shows that coaching can substantially improve the performance of individuals, which then leads to better business results at the organisational level as well.[16] When you coach every day you can amplify those results for huge benefits.

Tom Peters, expert of business management practices, says, 'Management is about arranging and telling. Leadership is about nurturing and enhancing.' When you coach every day you are participating in nurturing your team.

So the more you can coach, the more you can ask questions and help them each day. But this takes a system. The systems you implement will depend on your unique practice or business and your team structure. But having a system means you are not having to think of everything.

One technique you can use is something like the GROW Model which was originally developed by business coaches Graham Alexander, Alan Fine and Sir John Whitmore. GROW stands for:

- Goal
- Current Reality

---

[16] Roša, A & Lace, N. (December 2021). 'Assessment of the Impact of Coaching on a Company's Performance: A Review of Methods.' *Journal of Open Innovation: Technology, Market, and Complexity*. Available at https://www.sciencedirect.com/science/article/pii/S2199853122001731.

- Options (or Obstacles)
- Will (or Way Forward).[17]

Using this you can help your team to find a goal, determine where they are, consider where they want to go and look for ways to get there. Asking them what you can do to help or what they might need from you will help them to feel supported in meeting those goals.

To ensure that you're coaching every day, set up methods or times when you can be available to your team. Setting up a single time limits the amount of disruptions that will happen in your own work. In addition, schedule in regular times to chat more officially, providing feedback and coaching in a more official manner.

Spell it out

Whenever you're communicating with your team – whether it's through your regular coaching or simple daily task assignments – it's important that you really spell out what you are looking for. One of the most common issues that I see in leaders is that we expect our teams to know what we mean, what we agree on and how we work. But that is not generally the case.

Stephen Covey found in his research that 60% of people are dealing with unclear expectations.[18] This creates problems in the business, including procrastination and friction, because it stops things flowing. It means that people aren't clear on what they're going to do, so they just don't do it.

---

[17] 'The GROW Model of Coaching and Mentoring: A Simple Process for Developing Your People.' Mind Tools. Available at https://www.mindtools.com/an0fzpz/the-grow-model-of-coaching-and-mentoring.

[18] Covey. The 7 Habits of Highly Effective People.

In order to introduce more clarity, you have to spell it out. That means being really clear in your processes, tasks, systems and communications, so that your team can be very clear about your expectations.

It's like putting on a pair of glasses. Without them everything can be really a bit vague and unclear. But when you are clear in your communications – when you spell out exactly what you want when you want it – then it's like being able to really see for the first time.

Don't be put off when you have to deliver some negative feedback or constructive criticism. As Brené Brown says, 'Clear is kind.' And that's because the more clarity your team has, the easier it is for them to meet your expectations. This feels good, and creates more opportunities for them to be more high-performing and well connected.

Patrick Lencioni, in his book *The Advantage*, talks about how to bring together a high-performing and well-connected team for a high-performing organisation. He says that what you as a leader need to become is the chief reminder officer. This means that you need to repeat your messages. You need to be really clear, and you need to be really repetitive.[19]

To understand where you are not being clear for your team, look to where there is friction and unmet expectations. Is it in your processes, procedures, brochures, white papers, landing pages or websites? Is it in your collateral or how you give feedback? Or it might be in contracts.

Then determine what you need to do to be clearer. Where you can repeat yourself so that the team really hears and understands what you are expecting. Once you have determined these, add to your workflow and tasks the processes that support that clarity. Do you need to add a

---

[19] Lencioni, P. (2012). The Advantage: Why Organizational Health Trumps Everything Else In Business (J-B Lencioni Series). Jossey-Bass.

separate task for each project where you outline the requirements a second time? Or perhaps they outline it back to you?

Whatever the steps are that allow you to speak to them clearly and reiterate it again, build those in. This clarity will show that you do really care and that you are there to help nurture your team in their growth? And one of those systems could be the daily huddles.

Daily huddles

Imagine this. You've woken up lacking motivation and energy for the day. You head into the dining room – and there's your family, gathered around the table, sharing breakfast.

They are discussing the day ahead, the challenges they may face and the goals they hope to achieve.

You share your emotions, and feel seen and heard.

This infectious energy turns your mood around and you leave that family breakfast feeling connected and excited for the day ahead.

When it comes to your practice, your daily huddle is a lot like sharing breakfast with your family. When you run it effectively, it can lead to feelings of connection, loyalty and growth. And that has a huge amount of value for your team.

We've just been talking about the daily debrief, but the daily huddle has a different function. In fact, it's just a colloquial way to refer to a daily check-in or planning meeting for your team. It is widely acknowledged to be a system for communicating expectations for the day, giving feedback, answering questions and measuring the progress of a team's work.

Why do we need daily huddles?

We've all seen the amusing, 'this meeting could have been an email' meme. It went viral because so many of us can relate. Far too often, we feel like we're wasting our time sitting in a meeting that leads nowhere. But that's generally because the meetings themselves are inefficient and poorly handled.

On the other hand, an efficient and useful meeting can make a huge difference to you and your staff. Meetings are vital for leaders striving to keep people connected during times of growth and change. And they are equally important for people who need support and answers so they can do their job to the best of their capabilities.

As we discussed above, if your team doesn't know what's expected of them, they simply can't fulfil those expectations. The daily huddle is a fantastic way to check in with your team and convey your expectations.

I recently met with a client who was telling me she was unhappy with a new member of her team. Even after 90 days with this employee, she was only rating her at a three. After that long, I would expect her to be around a six or a seven.

So I asked the client, 'Are you doing daily huddles?'

She replied that she was doing them once a week. So over those 90 days, she'd had 12 chances to connect with her new staff member. However, if she had conducted daily huddles, she would have had more than 60 opportunities to work with her.

More than 60 opportunities to convey her expectations. More than 60 opportunities to give feedback. And more than 60 opportunities to help her employees take initiative.

And that would have led to higher performance from her team.

When I suggested that she switch to daily huddles in order to help her employee thrive, she was initially very reluctant. She told me that she simply didn't have enough time on the work day to conduct a daily huddle. She had clients to see and workshops to set up. A daily meeting just felt like too much.

But I told her that all she really needed was just 15 minutes. The important thing is fitting it in every single day.

We brainstormed when she could possibly fit them in and found that she could conduct a daily huddle on the drive to her workshops. Because by managing her own time to fit in the daily meeting, she was also demonstrating to her staff how to manage their time to accomplish their tasks. And by setting expectations they became better at managing their time and focusing on the important things each day.

I had another client who came into our community who felt that she was doing too much on her own. At this time she was going through extreme change post-COVID – and managing the changes in her practice that came along with that was taking up far too much of her time.

I suggested that she implement a daily huddle with her team. This gave her the opportunity to speak to her team daily, and outsource the things that were taking up her time. It also allowed her to flexibly respond to the changes that were coming through daily.

The outcome was that she was able to get more out of her team every day. And they were able to ride out a changing environment much more easily.

Your daily huddle helps you get the most out of your team, especially during times of change.

When it comes to growing your business, a daily huddle is a necessity. You have to be able to show your staff how to manage the changes that come from growth. You have to be there to answer questions and provide feedback. And you need to be able to step them through what needs to be done on a daily basis to manage your growth for a sustainable business.

As Steve Jobs said, 'Great things are never done by one person. They're done by a team of people.' The daily huddle gives you your chance to really bring your team online in your practice. And that can only mean more success for each of your team members, you and your practice overall.

If you want to run an effective daily huddle, you must set the standard. Consider sharing the following expectations with your team:

- Come prepared for the meeting, including any questions they might have. This encourages more productivity.
- Expect to be asked what the focus is for the day ahead.
- Be prepared to receive feedback and coaching.

Debrief daily

When we go to the doctor, they'll identify what our problem is and give us a diagnosis. Then they'll give us a solution, which is often a prescription, and sometimes say, 'Come back in two weeks so I can see how you're going.' Having a follow-up appointment with the doctor allows us to make sure that we are improving, that we've got better. They check in on us to make sure that everything is working.

We need to have a similar approach in our businesses and practices. Without a reflective practice we aren't able to ensure that what we have implemented does work, or review what actually hasn't worked. For every project and program we release, for every change we implement into our practice, we have to ask, 'has it solved the problem?' If it has, great. If it hasn't, what do we need to change in our course of action?

This reflective practice needs to be built into our practice. And we can do this by debriefing with our team every day.

I love the book *On Time On Target: How teams and companies can cut through complexity and get things done...the fighter pilot way*. In it the authors talk about how pilots debrief after every flight. They talk to their teams about how it went – what went well and what didn't and, of course, what needs to be changed.[20] Since they do it after every single flight, this helps them to continually improve, a vital element in their line of work. This is their version of the daily debrief.

I have a client that's had a practice for some time, and she's never had the luxury of a team – and because of that she's never had the luxury of daily debriefs. So one of the things that I implemented in her practice was to ensure that every single program that she delivers, whether it's a keynote, a workshop or some other client work, is that she completes a debrief with the client and the client's team each time. This led to her gaining more insight into what was working well in her delivery, and what wasn't. And she was able to start making changes to support her continuous improvement as well.

When you are able to debrief daily in your own practice, you will also be able to harness that process of continuous improvement. This might only be 1% of your work day, but it will lead to exponential growth in your performance and commitment to excellence, not just for yourself but for your entire team as well. In fact, research shows that well-conducted debriefs can improve team effectiveness by up to 25% regardless of the organisation or industry.[21]

So how do you implement a system of daily debriefs? Plan for the debrief at the start of your project and then allocate time after it's happened. If you wait until some situation arises that needs to be dealt

---

[20] Murphy, J & Boucousis, C. (2016). On Time On Target: How teams and companies can cut through complexity and get things done...the fighter pilot way. Allen & Unwin.

[21] Allen, J, Reiter-Palmon, R, Crowe, J & Scott, C. (2018). 'Debriefs: Teams Learning From Doing in Context.' University of Nebraska at Omaha: Department of Psychology. Available at https://digitalcommons.unomaha.edu/cgi/viewcontent.cgi?article=1200&context=psychfacpub.

with, and then decide to have a debrief, it's really too late. And if you don't prioritise it from the beginning, you'll just get too busy.

When you do have the debrief, you need to focus on how the project went. What were the best things? What were the worst things? And what needs to change? It doesn't need to be overcomplicated, but you do need to be disciplined to ensure that it happens. To do that you'll also need to make someone responsible for the daily debrief, to ensure it happens every single time.

If you want to debrief daily, you can also build this into your 15 minute daily huddle. Simply debrief on the work that went on the day before, and then take steps to remedy any issues or places of friction.

Plan your team members first 100 days

Real team care starts with individual team members. And your care for individual team members starts with your onboarding process – and that means planning their first 100 days.

John Maxwell, a *New York Times* bestselling author and leadership expert, once said, 'If you start today to do the right thing, you are already a success even if it doesn't show yet.' It can be hard in the first 100 days just to get someone going, and there can often be a delay in seeing strong, or even adequate, performance from new team members.

But if you take the time to get your new team members onboarded really well, it will pay off in dividends in the long term. You won't necessarily see the results immediately, but over time, it'll make a massive difference to how they perform.

I once delivered a course with a participant called Peter. He was frustrated because he was feeling really unhappy at work. And one of the key drivers was that he felt like he wasn't heard. This was exacerbated by the fact that his manager kept cancelling his meetings with him. This was particularly unfortunate because Peter was a new team member. He really needed to catch up with his manager weekly, in one-on-one, particularly in the first 100 days. Peter really wanted to contribute, but he just felt like he didn't really matter and that he wasn't really valued.

Getting the first 100 days right is like getting a boat on course. If your boat's a mere five degrees off course, over the length of your journey, you're going to end up a really long way out of range. The metaphor holds with our team members. If we are even slightly off in the first 100 days, then we can end up with a team member who ends up really off course in our own organisation.

On the other hand, if you can get that first 100 days right, then you're going to stay right on course, and your team members will have the opportunity to get to the right place in the end.

Joey Coleman has written a really great book called *Never Lose an Employee Again*. And it's all about what to do in those first 100 days to stop just doing the bare minimum to get your new team member started and to start investing in the onboarding elements that will really set them up for success for the long term. Part of his eight phases of the employee journey includes how to better onboard a client – and he says you need to start by creating a greeting on the first day that they'll be talking about years later.[22]

So when you start planning the first 100 days of your team member's work with you, start by asking yourself what you should do on the first day? How will you awe your new team member, and make their integration into the team feel good? Then put in the steps for what you should do during the first week, then month, then quarter and then even year.

---

[22] Coleman, J. (2023). Never Lose an Employee Again: The Simple Path to Remarkable Retention. Portfolio.

Then determine how you will communicate those things? Will you make phone calls or have meetings? If so, when? What are the indicators that you're looking for to show you need to take the next steps? And how are you setting the tone for the rest of their employment?

Every business or practice will be different. But by mapping your team member's first 100 days, and planning your processes for integration into the wider team, you'll be setting them up for incredible success – and your own business as well.

Check in on team each day

We already know that it's important to pay attention to our team, reach out daily and ask them how they are. When you're working with your team, whether it's face-to-face or online, ensure you check in each day, even if it's just to say, 'Do you need anything from me today?'

This needs to be a system. It needs to be part of your daily to-do list, that goes beyond just noticing your team's facial expressions and body language, or being interested in how they are doing… really. This needs to be a part of the process of your practice because when you check in on your team everyday they know that they're on your mind, that you care and that they matter.

This is particularly important if you're mostly remote. It's really easy to get busy, and if you're not seeing people in the office that day, it can be as simple as 'out of sight, out of mind'. But it doesn't take much to send a text or a message just to say, hey and let them know that you're there if they need anything. We want to make sure they know that they're an important part of the team.

When you check in each day, it feels a little bit like being under a warm blanket. It helps them to feel safe and secure. And research shows that when you've got a high level of trust and psychological safety, you can create change and drive performance.[23]

Gavin Larkin created R U OK? Day, a non-profit suicide prevention organisation. R U OK? Day is the day where we are challenged to ask others if they are OK? While R U OK? Day is really about mental health and wellbeing, the importance of checking in is something that matters for every person in every walk of life. And when you do check in with your team, it will help their mental health by making them feel valued.

The people that make up your team will impact how often they come to you for help. At the moment we have five different generations in the workplace, who will all respond differently when something goes wrong. With some people you may never hear about problems in their lives – particularly if you're not checking in, while others – generally the younger generations – may reach out for support and help a bit earlier.

As a leader, your own generation mah impact how often you decide to check in on people. But this is actually the wrong approach – because your timing may be much different than a specific team member. Instead, you need to build in the process of checking in so that you can pick things up a little bit earlier when perhaps there might be something wrong.

I used to have a boss when I worked in a workplace and she would come in in the mornings and she would walk past the entire team and not even say hello. We knew she was busy, but not having her acknowledge us took a toll. And it wouldn't have taken much for her to just say, 'Hi everyone.' Better yet, would be if she stopped in to check with each of

---

[23] Delizonna, L. (2017). 'High-Performing Teams Need Psychological Safety: Here's How to Create It, Six ways to build trust.' *Harvard Business Review*. Available athttps://hbr.org/2017/08/high-performing-teams-need-psychological-safety-heres-how-to-create-it.

us. Instead she had a missed opportunity each morning just to find out how we were going, and get the temperature and vibe of the team.

For us as leaders, that's really our job. It's our job to support and lead and create an environment to help our teams get through any stresses and situations that they're trying to get through while providing them with opportunities for learning and growth. And a daily check in can be a great step to getting there.

Make it a point – part of your system – to check in on your team each day. A quick text or message saying, 'How are you going? What are you working on?' or 'How can I help?' And even just those simple three questions. Your business and practice will benefit immensely if you can just simply check in, acknowledge people, see if they're OK and support them when they're not.

Conclusion

Your team is the heart and soul of your business. Caring for and nurturing them needs to be a priority if you want your business to succeed. Putting the effort in to know your team, to reach out and check in, to coach and support will make a huge amount of difference to the loyalty you get back. And that will make a huge difference to the success of your business overall.

CHAPTER 7

IN CLOSING

This book covers a lot of ground about how to make care your competitive advantage – from having a nurturing mindset to defining your approach to self-care, customer care and team care. The concepts in the book are designed to start the conversation and inspire you rather than make you feel overwhelmed. They're designed to help you consider how they may apply for you, your team and organisation, as well as what else builds your brand and the trust, connection and influence you have on the people who matter in your world.

The ideas behind this book and the platform will help give you a framework to consider, measure and gain insights into the areas where you have strengths and other areas where there might be an opportunity to improve. As you improve each area you'll experience a continuous leveling up, whether it's each day, quarter or year as you make more conscious and intentional choices around care and begin building a culture of care in your business.

The key to remember is not to be afraid to start small. Whilst learning to become a nurturing leader may seem like a huge mountain to climb, it can just start with you taking a single step. One conversation, one idea at a time. Take the lead and be the example that others can follow. From there the ripple of change begins that will ultimately lead you closer and closer to becoming exceptional every single day.

I would love to hear how you go implementing these strategies and striving towards making care your competitive advantage. Please reach out to share your stories and examples to me at jane@jane-anderson.com.au.

I'm cheering you on!

Work with Jane

In a world of constant change, there is a greater need for consultants and experts in their fields to lead and help their clients navigate change. To do this they need a highly influential personal brand, catalyst content and effective business support to build their tribe.

With over 25 years experience and named as one of the top three branding experts in the world, Jane has helped over 150,000 people to build their identity and influence. She is a certified speaker, coach and has been featured on *Sky Business*, *The Today Show*, *The Age*, *Sydney Morning Herald*, *BBC* and *Management Today*. The author of 11 books, Jane typically speaks at conferences, runs workshops, consults and coaches. She also has a particular focus on female leaders helping them to build their personal brands, thought leadership and sales.

Jane holds one of the top 1% viewed LinkedIn profiles and is the host of the *Jane Anderson Show* podcast where she has interviewed modern thinkers such as Seth Godin.

She has also won over 45 marketing, business and coaching industry awards.

CORPORATE CLIENTS HAVE INCLUDED:

Telstra, International Rice Research Institute, Wesfarmers, Amadeus, Virgin Australia, IKEA, LEGO, Mercedes-Benz, Australian Medical Association, Shell Energy and Workcover.

Book in a time to chat here:
https://calendly.com/jane-0877/complimentary-discussion
or email Jane's team at support@jane-anderson.com.au or call the office at +61 7 3841 7772.

Alternatively jump on Jane's website at www.jane-anderson.com.au to find out about her workshops, speaking and coaching programs.

Other titles by Jane Anderson

Exceptionality

Women with Influence

Put Yourself out There

Catalyst Content

Personal Power Planner

Expert to Influencer

Connect

Trusted

Impact

Confidence

www.ingramcontent.com/pod-product-compliance
Lightning Source LLC
Chambersburg PA
CBHW072004290426
44109CB00018B/2122